# BLACK MUSIC

*Also by LeRoi Jones*

HOME: Social Essays
DUTCHMAN and THE SLAVE: Two Plays
BLUES PEOPLE: Negro Music in White America

# BLACK MUSIC

## LeRoi Jones

WILLIAM MORROW & COMPANY, INC.   ·   NEW YORK

# CONTENTS

# BLACK MUSIC

For John Coltrane
the heaviest spirit

# 1963

## Jazz and the White Critic

MOST JAZZ CRITICS have been white Americans, but most important jazz musicians have not been. This might seem a simple enough reality to most people, or at least a reality which can be readily explained in terms of the social and cultural history of American society. And it is obvious why there are only two or three fingers' worth of Negro critics or writers on jazz, say, if one understands that until relatively recently those Negroes who *could* become critics, who would largely have to come from the black middle class, have simply not been interested in the music. Or at least jazz, for the black middle class, has only comparatively recently lost some of its stigma (though by no means is it yet as popular among them as any vapid musical product that comes sanctioned by the taste of the white majority). Jazz was collected among the numerous skeletons the middle-class black man kept locked in the closet of his psyche, along with watermelons and gin, and whose rattling caused him no end of misery and self-hatred. As one Howard University philosophy professor said to me when I was an undergraduate, "It's fantastic how much bad taste the blues contain!" But it is just this "bad taste" that this Uncle spoke of that has been the one factor that has kept the best of Negro music from slipping sterilely into the echo chambers of middle-brow American culture. And to a great extent such "bad

taste" was kept extant in the music, blues or jazz because the
Negroes who were responsible for the best of the music,
were always aware of their identities as black Americans
and really did not, themselves, desire to become vague, fea-
tureless, Americans as is usually the case with the Negro
middle class. (This is certainly not to say that there have not
been very important Negro musicians from the middle class.
Since the Henderson era, their number has increased enor-
mously in jazz.

Negroes played jazz as they had sung blues or, even earlier, as they had shouted and hollered in those anonymous
fields, because it was one of the few areas of human expression available to them. Negroes who felt the blues, later jazz,
impulse, as a specific means of expression, went naturally
into the music itself. There were fewer social or extra-
expressive considerations that could possibly disqualify any
prospective Negro jazz musician than existed, say, for a
Negro who thought he might like to become a writer (or
even an elevator operator, for that matter). Any Negro who
had some ambition towards literature, in the earlier part of
this century, was likely to have developed so powerful an
allegiance to the sacraments of middle-class American culture that he would be horrified by the very idea of writing
about jazz.

There were few "jazz critics" in America at all until the
30's and then they were influenced to a large extent by what
Richard Hadlock has called "the carefully documented gee-
whiz attitude" of the first serious European jazz critics. They
were also, as a matter of course, influenced more deeply by
the social and cultural mores of their own society. And it is
only natural that their criticism, whatever its intention,
should be a product of that society, or should reflect at least
some of the attitudes and thinking of that society, even if not
directly related to the subject they were writing about,
Negro music.

Jazz, as a Negro music, existed, up until the time of the big bands, on the same socio-cultural level as the sub-culture from which it was issued. The music and its sources were *secret* as far as the rest of America was concerned, in much the same sense that the actual life of the black man in America was secret to the white American. The first white critics were men who sought, whether consciously or not, to understand this secret, just as the first serious white jazz musicians (Original Dixieland Jazz Band, Bix, etc.) sought not only to understand the phenomenon of Negro music but to appropriate it as a means of expression which they themselves might utilize. The success of this "appropriation" signaled the existence of an American music, where before there was a Negro music. But the white jazz musician had an advantage the white critic seldom had. The white musician's commitment to jazz, the *ultimate concern,* proposed that the sub-cultural attitudes that produced the music as a profound expression of human feelings, could be *learned* and need not be passed on as a secret blood rite. And Negro music is essentially the expression of an attitude, or a collection of attitudes, about the world, and only secondarily an attitude about the way music is made. The white jazz musician came to understand this attitude as a way of making music, and the intensity of his understanding produced the "great" white jazz musicians, and is producing them now.

Usually the critic's commitment was first to his *appreciation* of the music rather than to his understanding of the attitude which produced it. This difference meant that the potential critic of jazz had only to appreciate the music, or what he thought was the music, and that he did not need to understand or even be concerned with the attitudes that produced it, except perhaps as a purely sociological consideration. This last idea is certainly what produced the reverse patronization that is known as Crow Jim. The disparaging "all you folks got rhythm" is no less a stereotype, simply because it is proposed as a positive trait. But this Crow Jim attitude has not been as menacing or as evident a flaw in critical writing about jazz as has another manifestation of the white critic's failure to concentrate on the blues and jazz attitude rather than his conditioned appreciation of the music. The major flaw in this approach to Negro music is that it strips the music too ingenuously of its social and cultural intent. It seeks to define jazz as an art (or a folk art) that has come out of no intelligent body of socio-cultural philosophy.

We take for granted the social and cultural milieu and philosophy that produced Mozart. As western people, the socio-cultural thinking of eighteenth-century Europe comes to us as a history legacy that is a continuous and organic part of the twentieth-century West. The socio-cultural philosophy of the Negro in America (as a continuous historical phenomenon) is no less specific and no less important for any intelligent critical speculation about the music that came out of it. And again, this is not a plea for narrow sociological analysis of jazz, but rather that this music cannot be completely understood (in critical terms) without some attention to the attitudes which produced it. It is the philosophy of Negro music that is most important, and this philosophy is only partially the result of the sociological disposition of Negroes in America. There is, of course, much more to it than that.

Strict musciological analysis of jazz, which has come into favor recently, is also as limited as a means of jazz criticism as a strict sociological approach. The notator of any jazz solo, or blues, has no chance of capturing what in effect are the most important elements of the music. (Most transcriptions of blues lyrics are just as frustrating.) A printed musical example of an Armstrong solo, or of a Thelonius Monk solo, tells us almost nothing except the futility of formal musicology when dealing with jazz. Not only are the various jazz effects almost impossible to notate, but each note *means something* quite in adjunct to musical notation. The notes of a jazz solo exist in a notation strictly for musical reasons. The notes of a jazz solo, as they are coming into existence, exist as they do for reasons that are only concomitantly musical. Coltrane's cries are not "musical," but they *are* music and quite moving music. Ornette Coleman's screams and rants are only musical once one understands the music his emotional attitude seeks to create. This attitude is real, and perhaps the most singularly important aspect of his music. Mississippi Joe Williams, Snooks Eaglin, Lightnin' Hopkins have different emotional attitudes than Ornette Coleman, but all of these attitudes are continuous parts of the historical and cultural biography of the Negro as it has existed and developed since there was a Negro in America, and a music that could be associated with him that did not exist anywhere else in the world. The notes *means something;* and the something is, regardless of its stylistic considerations, part of the black psyche as it dictates the various forms of Negro culture.

Another hopeless flaw in a great deal of the writing about jazz that has been done over the years is that in most cases the writers, the jazz critics, have been anything but intellectuals (in the most complete sense of that word). Most jazz critics began as hobbyists or boyishly brash members of the American petit bourgeoisie, whose only claim to any understanding about the music was that they knew it was *different;* or else they had once been brave enough to make a trip into a Negro slum to hear their favorite instrumentalist defame Western musical tradition. Most jazz critics were (and are) not only white middle-class Americans, but middle-brows as well. The irony here is that because the majority of jazz critics are white middle-brows, most jazz criticism tends to enforce white middle-brow standards of excellence as criteria for performance of a music that in its most profound manifestations is completely antithetical to such standards; in fact, quite often is in direct reaction against them. (As an analogy, suppose the great majority of the critics of Western formal music were poor, "uneducated" Negroes?) A man can speak of the "heresy of bebop" for instance, only if he is completely unaware of the psychological catalysts that made that music the exact registration of the social and cultural thinking of a whole generation of black Americans. The blues and jazz aesthetic, to be fully understood, must be seen in as nearly its complete human context as possible. People made bebop. The question the critic must ask is: *why?* But it is just this *why* of Negro music that has been consistently ignored or misunderstood; and it is a question that cannot be adequately answered without first understanding the necessity of asking it. Contemporary jazz during the last few years has begun to take on again some of the anarchy and excitement of the bebop years. The cool and hard bop/funk movements since the 40's seem pitifully tame, even decadent, when compared to the music men like Ornette Coleman, Sonny Rollins, John Coltrane, Cecil Taylor and some others have been making recently. And of the bop pioneers, only Thelonius Monk has managed to maintain without question the vicious creativity with which he first entered the jazz scene back in the 40's. The music has changed again, for many of the same basic reasons it changed twenty years ago. Bop was, at a certain level of consideration, a reaction by young musicians against the sterility and formality of Swing as it moved to become a formal part of the mainstream American culture. The New Thing, as recent jazz has been called, is, to a large degree, a reaction to the hard bop-funk-groove-soul camp, which itself seemed to come into being in protest against the squelching of most of the blues elements in cool and progressive jazz. Funk (groove, soul) has become as formal and clichéd as cool or swing, and opportunities for imaginative expression within that form have dwindled almost to nothing.

The attitudes and emotional philosophy contained in "the new music" must be isolated and understood by critics before any consideration of the *worth* of the music can be legitimately broached. Later on, of course, it becomes relatively easy to characterize the emotional penchants that informed earlier aesthetic statements. After the fact, is a much simpler way to work and think. For example, a writer who wrote liner notes for a John Coltrane record mentioned how difficult it had been for him to appreciate Coltrane earlier, just as it had been difficult for him to appreciate Charlie Parker when he first appeared. To quote: "I wish I were one of those sages who can say, 'Man, I dug Bird the first time I heard him.' I didn't. The first time I heard Charlie Parker, I thought he was ridiculous . . ." Well, that's a noble confession and all, but the responsibility is still the writer's and in no way involves Charlie Parker or what he was trying to do. When that writer first heard Parker he simply did not understand *why* Bird should play the way he did, nor could it have been very important to him. But now, of course, it becomes almost a form of reverse snobbery to say that one did not think Parker's music was worth much at first hearing, etc. etc. The point is, it seems to me, that if the music is worth something now, it must have been worth something then. Critics are supposed to be people in a position to tell what is of value and what is not, and, hopefully, at the time it first appears. If they are consistently mistaken, what is their value?

Jazz criticism, certainly as it has existed in the United States, has served in a great many instances merely to obfuscate what has actually been happening with the music itself—the pitiful harangues that raged during the 40's between two "schools" of critics as to which was the "real jazz," the new or the traditional, provide some very ugly examples. A critic who praises Bunk Johnson at Dizzy Gillespie's expense is no critic at all; but then neither is a man who turns it around and knocks Bunk to swell Dizzy. If such critics

would (or could) reorganize their thinking so that they
begin their concern for these musicians by trying to understand why each played the way he did, and in terms of the
constantly evolving and redefined philosophy which has informed the most profound examples of Negro music
throughout its history, then such thinking would be impossible.

It has never ceased to amaze and infuriate me that in the
40's a European critic could be arrogant and unthinking
enough to inform serious young American musicians that
what they were feeling (a consideration that exists before,
and without, the music) was false. What had happened was
that even though the white middle-brow critic had known
about Negro music for only about three decades, he was
already trying to formalize and finally institutionalize it. It is
a hideous idea. The music was already in danger of being
forced into that junk pile of admirable objects and data the
West knows as *culture*.

Recently, the same attitudes have become more apparent
in the face of a fresh redefinition of the form and content of
Negro music. Such phrases as "anti-jazz" have been used to
describe musicians who are making the most exciting music
produced in this country. But as critic A. B. Spellman asked,
"What does anti-jazz mean and who are these ofays who've
appointed themselves guardians of last year's blues?" It is
that simple, really. What does anti-jazz mean? And who
coined the phrase? What is the definition of jazz? And who
was authorized to make one?

Reading a great deal of old jazz criticism is usually like
boning up on the social and cultural malaise that characterizes and delineates the bourgeois philistine in America. Even
rereading someone as intelligent as Roger Pryor Dodge in the
old *Record Changer* ("Jazz: its rise and decline," 1955) usually makes me either very angry or very near hysterical. Here
is a sample: ". . . let us say flatly that there is no future in

preparation for jazz through Bop . . . ," or, "The Boppists, Cools, and Progressives are surely stimulating a dissolution within the vagaries of a non-jazz world. The Revivalists, on the other hand have made a start in the right direction." It sounds almost like political theory. Here is Don C. Haynes in the April 22, 1946 issue of *Down Beat*, reviewing Charlie Parker's *Billie's Bounce* and *Now's The Time:* "These two sides are bad taste and ill-advised fanaticism. . . ." and, "This is the sort of stuff that has thrown innumerable impressionable young musicians out of stride, that has harmed many of them irreparably. This can be as harmful to jazz as Sammy Kaye." It makes you blush.

Of course there have been a few very fine writers on jazz, even as there are today. Most of them have been historians. But the majority of popular jazz criticism has been on about the same level as the quoted examples. Nostalgia, lack of understanding or failure to see the validity of redefined emotional statements which reflect the changing psyche of the Negro in opposition to what the critic might think the Negro ought to feel; all these unfortunate failures have been built many times into a kind of critical stance or aesthetic. An aesthetic whose standards and measure are connected irrevocably to the continuous gloss most white Americans have always made over Negro life in America. Failure to understand, for instance, that Paul Desmond and John Coltrane represent not only two very divergent ways of thinking about music, but more importantly two very different ways of viewing the world, is at the seat of most of the established misconceptions that are daily palmed off as intelligent commentary on jazz or jazz criticism. The catalysts and necessity of Coltrane's music must be understood as they exist even before they are expressed as music. The music is the result of the attitude, the stance. Just as Negroes made blues and other people did not because of the Negro's peculiar way of looking at the world. Once this attitude is delineated as a continuous though constantly evolving social philosophy directly attributable to the way the Negro responds to the psychological landscape that is his Western environment, criticism of Negro music will move closer to developing as consistent and valid an aesthetic as criticism in other fields of Western art.

There have been so far only two American playwrights, Eugene O'Neill and Tennessee Williams who are as profound or as important to the history of ideas as Louis Armstrong, Bessie Smith, Duke Ellington, Charlie Parker or Ornette Coleman, yet there is a more valid and consistent body of dramatic criticism written in America than there is a body of criticism about Negro music. And this is simply because there is an intelligent tradition and body of dramatic criticism, though it has largely come from Europe, that any intelligent American drama critic can draw on. In jazz criticism, no reliance on European tradition or theory will help at all. Negro music, like the Negro himself, is strictly an American phenomenon, and we have got to set up standards of judgment and aesthetic excellence that depend on our native knowledge and understanding of the underlying philosophies and local cultural references that produced blues and jazz in order to produce valid critical writing or commentary about it. It might be that there is still time to start.

# 1962

## Minton's

BY NOW it is almost impossible to find out just what did go on at Minton's during the early 40's. There are so many conflicting stories, many by people who have no way of knowing. But in my adolescence the myth went some-think like this: "Around 1942, after classical jazz had made its conquests, a small group used to get together every night in a Harlem night club called Minton's Playhouse. It was made up of several young colored boys who, unlike their fellow musicians, no longer felt at home in the atmosphere of 'swing music.' It was becoming urgent to get a little air in a richly decked out palace that was soon going to be a prison. That was the aim of trumpeter Dizzy Gillespie, pianist Thelonius Monk, guitarist Charlie Christian (who died before the group's efforts bore fruit), drummer Kenny Clarke and saxophonist Charlie Parker. Except for Christian, they were poor, unknown and unprepossessing: but Monk stimulated his partners by the boldness of his harmonies, Clarke created a new style of drum playing, and Gillespie and Parker took choruses that seemed crazy to the people who came to listen to them. The bebop style was in the process of being born."

It sounds almost like the beginnings of modern American writing among the emigrés of Paris. But this is the legend which filled most of my adolescence. However, as Thelonius Monk put it. "It's true modern jazz probably began to get popular there, but some of these histories and articles put what happened over the course of ten years into one year. They put people all together in one time in one place. I've seen practically everybody at Minton's, but they were just there playing. They weren't giving lectures."

Minton's opened in 1940 on 118th Street in the Hotel Cecil. Teddy Hill, the band leader, was running the place, and it was only natural that a lot of musicians would fall by whenever they got a chance. Even before the "bop" sessions got under way, musicians who were working up the street at the Apollo would come by after their last show, or even between shows, and sit in with whoever was on the stand. Mondays became the best night for open sessions, because a lot of musicians didn't have to go to their regular gigs. Charlie Christian used to cab it up from midtown, where he was working with Benny Goodman, after his last set and sit on the stand, no matter who was tooting, until four in the morning when the place was supposed to close. (When it did close musicians went further uptown to Monroe's.)

Lester Young, Coleman Hawkins, Ben Webster, Roy Eldridge and a lot of older musicians used to come in the place, too, although, one of the tales about Minton's is that Roy stopped coming in once Gillespie stopped imitating him and started blowing his own thing. Every night was cutting night, but Monday all the axes came out for real because the audiences were just about as hip as the musicians. In fact most of the audience, after a while, were musicians themselves.

There had to be a feeling of freedom and the excitement that goes with individual expression, because all of this began in the midst of the Swing Era, when the arranger, not the soloist was the important man in jazz. There were good soloists in the worst popular swing bands, yet even in the best bands, the arrangement wore the soloists like a Bellevue sport coat. But Minton's was where these young musicians could stand up and blow their brains out all night long, and experimentation led to innovation. A lot of musicians would leave Minton's after one of the Monday sessions claiming Monk, Bird, Dizzy, Klook and the others were purposely "playing weird," just so they could keep the bandstand to themselves.

Bop also carried with it a distinct element of social protest, not only in the sense that it was music that seemed antagonistically nonconformist, but also that the musicians who played it were loudly outspoken about who they thought they were. "If you don't like it, don't listen," was the attitude, which seems to me now as rational as you can get. These musicians seemed no longer to want to be thought of merely as "performers," in the old Cotton Club-yellow hiney sense, but as musicians. And this was an unforgivable change of emphasis for a great many people. Bebopper jokes were as common in the late 40's as were beatnik jokes recently. These Negro musicians were thought of as "weird" and "deep," the bebop glasses and goatees some wore seemed to complete the image.

About four years went by before any of the music that grew up in Minton's (and Monroe's) was heard by a great many people, because of the recording ban in effect at the time. Still the word got out, mouth to ear, that something really wiggy was brewing uptown. In 1944 when Gillespie and Parker started recording and working in some of the 52nd Street clubs, the whole jazz world got turned around, and the non-jazz world as well.

Today, Minton's is still full of sounds, though they are by no means "the new thing" or avant-garde. Usually, the groups that come into Minton's are stand-up replicas of what was highly experimental twenty-five years ago. These are groups that are now more "socially" acceptable, and make

up the mainstream of jazz, for the uptown mainstream listener.

The new jazz, for all intents and purposes, is centered
downtown on the lower eastside, in lofts, small bohemian-
type clubs, although there have been some efforts of late to
return the newest expression of the black soul back home.

# 1962

## The Dark Lady of the Sonnets

NOTHING WAS more perfect than what she was. Nor more willing to fail. (If we call failure something light can realize. Once you have seen it, or felt whatever thing she conjured growing in your flesh.)

At the point where what she did left singing, you were on your own. At the point where what she was was in her voice, you listen and make your own promises.

More than I have felt to say, she says always. More than she has ever felt is what we mean by fantasy. Emotion, is wherever you are. She stayed in the street.

The myth of blues is dragged from people. Though some others make categories no one understands. A man told me Billie Holiday wasn't singing the blues, and he knew. O.K., but what I ask myself is what had she seen to shape her singing so? What, in her life, proposed such tragedy, such final hopeless agony? Or flip the coin and she is singing, "Miss Brown To You." And none of you cats would dare cross her. One eye closed, and her arms held in such balance, as if all women were so aloof. Or could laugh so.

And even in the laughter, something other than brightness, completed the sound. A voice that grew from a singer's instrument to a woman's. And from that (those last records critics say are weak) to a black landscape of need, and perhaps, suffocated desire.

Sometimes you are afraid to listen to this lady.

# 1963

## Recent Monk

*TIME* MAGAZINE'S cover of the 25th of November 1963 was scheduled to be a portrait of Thelonius Monk. But when President Kennedy was assasinated, another cover was substituted. The Monk cover was also to be accompanied by a rather long *Time* magazine specialty biography which was supposed to present Monk, at long last, to polite society, officially.*

One thinks immediately of another jazz musician to be so presented, Dave Brubeck, and even though it seems to be impossible that Monk could ever even think to receive the kind of "acceptance," and with that, the kind of loot that Brubeck received because of his canonization, it did not seem too extreme an optimism to predict the swelling of Monk's bank account, etc., as a result of such exposure, though it was not certain the cover would ever appear. But the very fact that such a cover was scheduled does mean that Monk's fortunes are definitely still rising. The idea of seeing Thelonius Monk's face on a cover of *Time* magazine would have seemed, only a few years ago, like a wild joke. As a matter of fact, seeing a dummy cover, as I did, my first reaction was that someone was trying to put you on. I'm still not absolutely sure they didn't.

* The cover finally did appear, February 1964.

But what remains puzzling, though not completely, is the reasons for such a step by the Luceforce. What can it possibly mean? (Aw, man, it means they figure they got to be *au courant*, like everybody else.) One understands *Time* promoting a man like Brubeck, who can claim jazz fugues and American college students to his credit, the wholesome cultural backdrop of which would certainly sit well with the *Time* editors who could project Brubeck into the homes of their readers as a genius of New Culture. But even taking into consideration Monk's widening acceptance by jazz tastemakers, and even the passing of his name around a growing audience merely by his Columbia recordings, it is still a wondrous idea that people at *Time*, hence, a pretty good swath of that part of the American population called "knowledgeable," now have some idea they can connect with Thelonius Monk.

And what, finally, does that mean? Has Monk finally been allowed onto the central dais of popular culture? If such is the case, one wonders why not put Miles Davis' picture on that magazine, since it is certain that after his last few Columbia efforts, Davis has definitely entered the larger marketplace. But Monk is Columbia property, too, and equally available through the record club, etc. That is, his music is now open to the most casual of tastes. But then, so is Mozart's.

I don't think the truism about success being more difficult to handle than failure is entirely useless. Certainly almost everyone must have some example, and within the precincts of American Jazz, of some artist or performer who, once he had made it safely to the "top," either stopped putting out or began to imitate himself so dreadfully that early records began to have more value than new records or in-person appearances. There are hosts of men like this, in all fields, around America. It is one of this country's specialties.

So Monk, someone might think taking a quick glance, has really been set up for something bad to happen to his play-

ing. He came into the Five Spot for what turned out to be a
six-month stay. That fact alone could have turned some
musicians off just as easily, i.e., the boring grind such a long
date might turn out to be, especially perhaps under the
constant hammer of slightly interested audiences—the presence of which, in any club, is one symbol of that club's
success.

But Monk is much harder than any of these possible de-
tractions from his art. He is an old man, in the sense of
having facts at his disposal any pianist, or man, for that
matter, might learn something from. *Down Beat* says that
Bill Evans is the most influential pianist of the moment.* I
would suppose, by that, that they mean in their editorial offices. Monk's influence permeates the whole of jazz by now,
and certainly almost none of the younger wizards just beginning to unfold, and even flower, have completely escaped
Thelonius' facts. Young musicians like Cecil Taylor, Archie
Shepp, Ornette Coleman, Don Cherry, Eric Dolphy and so
many others acknowledge and constantly demonstrate their
large debt to Monk. In fact, of all the bop greats, Monk's influence seems second now only to that of Charlie Parker
among the younger musicians.

Even though Monk should be considered a jazz master,
having piled up his credits since the early days of yesteryear,
viz., at Minton's and contributing to the innovations that
brought in the hard swing, it is only relatively recently that
some kind of general recognition has come his way. Even
though, for sure, there are still well-educated citizens who
must think of Monk (*Time* or not) as incomprehensible.
He's always had a strong reputation among musicians, but
perhaps his wider acceptance began during his stay at the
old Five Spot the late spring and summer of 1957, with that
beautiful quartet consisting of John Coltrane, Wilbur Ware

* And still says it in '67.

and Shadow Wilson. Anyone who witnessed the transformation that playing with Monk sent John Coltrane through (opening night he was struggling with *all* the tunes), must understand the deepness and musical completeness that can come to a performer under the Monk influence. It is not too far out to say that before the Monk job Trane was a very hip saxophonist, but after that experience, he had a chance to become a very great musician and an ubiquitous influence himself.

When Monk opened at the new Five Spot, the owners said that he would be there, "as long as he wanted." Monk also went out and bought a brand new piano, though after the long stay, there were hundreds of scratches, even gashes on the wood just above the keyboard, where Monk slashing at the keys, bangs the wood with his big ring, or tears it with his nails.

"No one," said Joe Termini, co-owner with his brother, Iggy, of the Five Spot, "draws crowds as consistently as Monk." And it seemed very true during the six months Monk spent at the new sleek version of the old Bowery jazz club. Most evenings there was a crowd of some proportions sitting around the club, and the weekends were always swinging and packed, the crowds stretching, sometimes, right out into the street. The crowds comprised of college students . . . by the droves, especially during the holidays . . . seasoned listeners, hippies, many musicians, tourists, explorers, and a not so tiny ungroupish group of people immediately familiar to each other, if perhaps obscure to others, Monkfans. For certain, a great many of the people who came and will come to see Monk come out of a healthy or unhealthy curiosity to see somebody "weird," as the mystique of this musician and his music, even as it has seeped down distorted, to a great extent, by the cultural lag into the more animated fringe of the mainstream culture, has led them to believe he is.

Of course many of Monk's actions can be said to be

strange . . . they are, but they are all certainly his own. He is
a very singular figure, wearing a stingy brim version of a Rex
Harrison hat every night I saw him for the whole stretch of
the date. All the old stories about Monk coming hours late
for a job and never being able to hold a gig dissipated at the
Five Spot to a certain extent. Certainly a six-month stand, if
not the shorter stand at the old Five Spot, ought to prove he
can hold a job. And after a while Monk kept adjusting his
employers and his audience to his entrance times, and while
someone might think, if it was his first time in the Spot, that
the music should begin a little earlier, anyone who had been
through those changes before, and gotten used to the
schedule, knew that Thelonius never got there until around
eleven. But he was very consistent about that.

Monk's most familiar routine at the Five Spot, was to
zoom in just around eleven and head straight back for the
kitchen, and into some back room where he got rid of his
coat and then walked quickly back out into the club and
straight to the bar. Armed with a double bourbon "or something," he would march very quickly up to the bandstand
and play an unaccompanied solo. This would be something
like "Crepuscule With Nellie" or "Ruby My Dear" or a very
slow and beautiful "Don't Blame Me," the last finished off
most times with one of his best "James P. Johnson" tinkles.

After the solo, Monk would take the microphone and an-
nounce (which surprised even the Monkfans who by now
have grown used to the pianist's very close-mouthed de-
meanor on the stand). But the announcements, for the
most part, were very short: something like, "And now,
Frankie Dunlop will play you some tubs." Then Monk would
disappear out into the alcove, and a few fans who had
waited for a long time, say a couple hours, to hear Thelonius,
would groan very audibly, but would still have to wait for a
while longer until the rest of the program was finished. After
Dunlop's unaccompanied drum solo Monk would return to

the stand, but only to say, "Butch Warren will play a bass solo," and gesturing toward Warren as he left the stand, returning to the alcove to walk back and forth or dance with the solo, he'd add, "You got it!" "Softly as in the Morning Sunrise" was what Warren usually played.

Finally, the entire group would come onto the stand together, Dunlop on drums, Warren the bassist and tenor saxophonist Charlie Rouse. Many many nights, the first tune the group did jointly was "Sweet and Lovely," which began as a slow Monkish ballad, only to take wings behind Charlie Rouse's breathy swing and easy lyricism. Before the night was over one was likely to hear that tune three or four times, but it never got wearing. An average set was likely to be comprised of about four tunes, maybe, "Rhythm-a-ning," "Criss Cross," "Blue Monk," ending each set with "Epistrophy." But almost everything heard thoughout any given evening was a Monk piece, except for the few standards like "Tea For Two," "Sweet Georgia Brown," "Don't Blame Me," which upon hearing seem immediately and permanently transformed into Monk originals. But mostly he played tunes like "Misterioso," "Straight, No Chaser," "Off Minor," "Well You Needn't," "I Mean You," "Evidence," and other of his own now well-known compositions.

The group, by now, is very much a tightly connected musical unit. They have a unison sound that is unmistakable and usually the ensemble playing is close to impeccable. Monk and Rouse are the soloists, though each player did take a solo on almost each tune, and sometimes the other two players, Warren and Dunlop, did come up with a striking solo, but most times the solo force had to be carried by Monk and Rouse. (Dunlop is a light, occasionally dazzling, tapdancer of a drummer, who barely seems to touch the skins: Warren is a very young, very promising bass player who is still looking to find his way completely out of the Oscar Peterson bag.) Charlie's playing is almost artifact-like at times, sometimes detrimentally so, but when Monk was knifing through his polished dialogues with sharp, sometimes bizarre-sounding chords . . . always right though . . . then Rouse was stampeded into making something really exciting, for all his insouciant elegance. One night on "Criss Cross" this happened and Charlie went off into tenor saxophone heaven, he was tooting so hard.

But sometimes one wishes Monk's group wasn't so polished and impeccable, and that he had some musicians with him who would be willing to extend themselves a little further, dig a little deeper into the music and get out there somewhere near where Monk is, and where his compositions always point to.

Monk's playing is still remarkable. The things he can do and does do almost any night, even when he's loafing, are just out of sight. Even when he's just diddling around the keys looking for a chord to shake somebody . . . the rest of his group most times . . . up, he makes a very singularly exciting music. Critics who talk about this pianist's "limited technical abilities" (or are there any left?) should really be read out of the club. Monk can get around to any place on the piano he thinks he needs to be, and for sheer piano-lesson brilliance, he can rattle off arpeggios and brilliant sizzling runs that ought to make even those "hundred finger" pianists take a very long serious look.

While the other musicians solo, Monk usually gets up from the piano and does his "number," behind the piano, occasionally taking a drink. The quick dips, half-whirls, and deep pivoting jerks that Monk gets into behind that piano are part of the music, too. Many musicians have mentioned how they could get further into the music by watching Monk dance, following the jerks and starts, having dug that that was the emphasis Monk wanted on the tune. He would also skip out into the alcove behind the bandstand, and continue the dance, and from the bar it was pretty wiggy digging Monk stepping and spinning, moving back and forth just beyond the small entrance to the stand. You'd see only half a movement, or so, and then he'd be gone off to the other side, out of sight.

One evening after the last tune of the set, Monk leaped up from the bench, his hands held in the attitude he had assumed as he finished the number, and without changing that attitude (hands up and in front of him as he lifted them from the keys) he wheeled off the stand and did a long drawn out shuffle step from the stand completely around the back of the club. Everyone in the club stopped, sort of, and followed him with their eyes, till he had half circled the entire club. Monk brought the semicircle to a stop right at the center of the bar, and without dropping his attitude or altering his motion he called out to the bartender, very practically and logically, "Give me a drink." Somebody next to me said, to no one in particular, "Now, you get to that."

Monk goes on as he does, playing very beautifully, very often, and at least giving out piano lessons the rest of the time. (The last set of the evening, he would usually get into the remarkable part of his skills, and for some reason, when the club was down to its last serious drinkers and serious listeners, he, and the rest of the group because they sensed the leader's feelings, would get way up and scare most of us.)

Monk is a success now, and there's no getting around it, nor should there be, because he's one person and musician who deserves it very much. He's paid more dues real and mythological than most musicians are ever faced with paying. As a matter of fact, even at the height of his success at the Five Spot, Monk had to go downtown one day, and go through still more changes with the cabaret card people, and the word was that the whole routine wasn't really necessary and that those worthies just took Monk through the thing because they could. But Monk now is making his way into bigtime America, and he hasn't given his mind away on the way in. He's still "out there," and showing no signs of becoming anything other than what he's been for quite a long time now.

The last night at the Spot, I asked him when he was coming back. (Charlie Mingus replaced him.) He said, "You never can tell."

# 1963

## Three Ways to Play the Saxophone

I THINK there are very few people who are close to jazz who would dispute the fact that the three most important saxophonists in all jazz history, up to now, have been Coleman Hawkins, Lester Young and Charlie Parker. There have, of course, been other important jazz saxophonists, but these three men have been more than just brilliant instrumentalists and gifted improvisors; what is most important is that they were innovators, and lasting influences on their contemporaries and every other jazz musician to come after them, no matter what instrument they might play. Just as you once could find (and can still find) piano players or guitarists who patterned their styles on what Louis Armstrong did on trumpet, so you can find diverse instrumentalists making curious, or not so curious, uses of what *Bean*, *Pres* and *Bird* have done. Charlie Parker's influence is just as important to post-bop piano players as it is to saxophonists. Even a musician as patently individual as vibist, Milt Jackson, must admit to being heavily influenced by the Coleman Hawkins attack. There are guitar players and trombone players whose styles owe a great debt to Lester Young's behind-the-beat, *cool*, definition of jazz. But as far as jazz saxophone is concerned, it would be almost impossible to find a player who is untouched by what these three masters accomplished.

Of course the ways in which various saxophonists have used Parker's or Hawkins' or Young's influence, have differed quite widely. There are saxophonists who are merely content to imitate, almost exactly, or as closely as they are able, the style of one of the innovators. But the most imaginative hornmen are always able to maintain enough of their own personalities so that any use they make of, say, a Lester Young, is interesting, and even moving, in its own right. Also, there are many very fine players who have been able to utilize two of the major styles at the same time and still come up with something beautifully singular. One thinks immediately of a tenor man like Lucky Thompson who seems to have understood both Hawkins and Young equally, and to have arrived at an astonishingly original use of both those antithetical concepts of tenor saxophone playing. Gene Ammons is another fine tenor player who puts both Young and Hawkins to work in his own playing and manages to emerge as a fascinating stylist. Charlie Rouse, yet another. And, of course, there are many more. The point is that for every Paul Quinichette, say, who was content to utilize merely Lester Young's heavy influence, or Sonny Stitt, who could hear only Parker, or Chu Berry, who was fastened to Hawkins, there were other players who were able to take some of the strongest qualities of two of the innovators, or even all three, after bebop and the emergence of Charlie Parker as the third giant of the jazz saxophone, and fashion their own personal styles.

It is possible to trace the development and ascendancy of the saxophone in jazz by citing just what each of these three men contributed. Coleman Hawkins is known by most jazz people as "The Man Who Invented The Saxophone." It was Bean who first made the sax a respectable instrument, as far as jazz musicians were concerned. Before his appearance, the instrument was used largely for its novelty effect in dance bands and those hotel or theatre groups known as

"Mickey Mouse" bands. Hawkins took the horn, and inspired by Louis Armstrong's trumpet technique, developed a huge tone and a smooth, on-the-beat approach to saxophone phrasing that brought the instrument into its own as a jazz solo voice. And for a long time after Hawkins almost anyone who played the instrument sounded like him . . . there was just no other way.

Lester (Pres) Young brought the tenor saxophone to perhaps an even more autonomous position as a solo instrument. Instead of emulating Hawkins' wide-toned, on-the-beat, eighth-note approach, Pres, inspired as he said by the C-melody saxophone of Frank Traumbauer, brought a light, flowing, gauzy tone to the tenor. He also liked to lag just a little behind the beat and accent this penchant by "laying out" or resting at then unusual places in a phrase, and then swooping lazily but impeccably back into the phrase as if he had never stopped playing. Hawkins' saxophone work, as impressive as it was, was really just an extension of the Louis Armstrong trumpet style to another instrument. But Young made for the first time a music that was strictly a "saxophone music," and his flexible, almost uncanny, rhythmic sense provided a model for many of the young musicians who came along in the 40's to produce the music called bebop. Since Young, jazz has become increasingly a saxophone music, in the sense that the music's chief innovators since that time have been saxophonists. From the earliest days of jazz the chief solo instrument had been the trumpet, and trumpet players like the fabled Buddy Bolden, Freddy Keppart, King Oliver and Louis Armstrong, the music's most illustrious soloists. But Hawkins demonstrated how powerfully jazz could be played on a saxophone, and Young made the saxophone potentially the music's most expressive instrument.

Alto saxophonist, Charlie Parker was one of the two most exciting soloists jazz has seen so far; the other, of course, being Louis Armstrong. And as such, he made jazz musicians even more saxophone conscious. After Parker, trumpet players, piano players, guitar players, bass players, etc., all tried to sound like him, in much the same fashion as all kinds of instrumentalists had once tried to sound like Armstrong. Parker made the conquest of the music by the saxophone, which Young had begun, very nearly complete. Since Young, we have had Roy Eldridge, Dizzy Gillespie, Fats Navarro, Miles Davis, Clifford Brown, all as brilliant trumpet soloists, but the chief innovators have been saxophonists. And just as Parker was the soul and fire of the bebop era (in fact, most jazz saxophonists are even now heavily indebted to him), it is still saxophonists who are the fiercest innovators in contemporary jazz.

Right at this moment (in 1963) three of the most daring innovators in jazz are saxophone players. And a curious coincidence is that like Hawkins, Young and Parker, the proportion remains the same, i.e., two tenor saxophonists and one alto player make up the triumvirate. The tenor men are Sonny Rollins and John Coltrane. The alto player is Ornette Coleman, the most controversial of the three.

Of the three, Rollins has been on the jazz scene the longest, having come up with the "second generation" of boppers. Rollins, like everyone else of the period, was deeply affected by Charlie Parker's music, and his style on tenor has always shown Parker's influence. But by the mid-fifties Rollins came into his own and began to play his own horn, and since then he has become an extremely ubiquitous influence himself. In fact Rollins was perhaps the strongest voice of the recent *Hard Bop* trend. It was a trend that was marked by a "return" by many jazz musicians to what they considered their roots (as a reaction to the soft timbres and rigid arrangements of cool jazz). Saxophonists began to utilize wider and harsher tones, of which Sonny's was the widest and harshest and most expressive, and accompanying piano chords became more basic and simplified, often relying on a sort of gospel or *churchy* feeling to emphasize the Afro-American beginnings of the music. This trend still persists in what is called *soul music* or *funky* jazz, which is still enjoying a great deal of popularity. But Rollins has since gone on to deeper and even more expressive things. Albums like *Way Out West, Freedom Suite* and *Saxophone Colossus* showed that Sonny was interested in being more than fashionable. And he still had more experimenting to do.

John Coltrane, after playing with various rhythm and blues groups, and one of Dizzy Gillespie's big bands late in the 40's, began to be noticed in the middle 50's as a member of the Miles Davis Quartet and Quintet. Coltrane's biggest influence for quite a while was Dexter Gordon, who also influenced Rollins and was one of the earliest people to transfer Parker's approach to the tenor saxophone. Coltrane was also struck quite a bit by Rollins, but by the time he finished playing with Thelonius Monk's wild groups (1957) he was well on his own way to becoming one of the most singular stylists in jazz.

The youngest of the three current saxophone innovators is alto man, Ornette Coleman. He is also the one whose innovations have been most challenged by many jazz critics and musicians whose shortsightedness makes it difficult for them to accept the genuinely new. Just as Young and Parker were for a long time considered charlatans or "merely inept," except by a few musicians and critics who tried to understand what they were doing, so young Coleman has had a difficult time of it, but he has been, to my mind, the most exciting and influential innovator in jazz since Parker. And even though Coleman didn't arrive on the "big time" jazz scene until 1959–60, he has already managed to influence, to quite an extent, the other two major innovators, Rollins and Coltrane, not to mention the myriads of other younger players, regardless of their instruments.

Rollins and Coltrane had mature styles before Ornette Coleman was known even to jazz "insiders." Rollins' huge tone, which often sounded like Coleman Hawkins paraphrasing Charlie Parker, and his ability to improvise logically and beautifully from thematic materials rather than chordal, were the things that characterized his pre-Coleman style. Coltrane's sound was and is smaller and less rigid than Rollins', and because of its striking similarity to a human cry it can often raise the hairs on the back of your neck. Rollins seems always to address himself to any extemporization in the most formally logical manner, while Coltrane strings seemingly endless notes and scales together, making what some critics called "sheets of sound."

Coltrane and Coleman have almost diametrically opposing approaches to a jazz solo. Coltrane's music takes its impetus and shape from the repeated chords that harmonically fix the tune. In fact, he plays sometimes as if he would like to take each note of a chord and sound it singly, but at the same time as the overall chord. It is like a painter who instead of painting a simple white, paints all the elemental pigments that the white contains, and at the same time as the white itself. But Ornette Coleman's music has been described as "non-chordal." That is, he does not limit his line to notes that are specifically called for by the sounded chord. The form of a Coleman solo is usually determined by the total musical shape of what he is playing, i.e., the melody, timbre, pitch and of course, the rhythm—all of these moved by Ornette's singularly emotional approach to jazz, in much the same way as the older, "primitive," blues singers produced their music. And this has been his largest influence on the two older men. This *freedom* that Coleman has insisted on in his playing, has opened totally fresh areas of expression for Coltrane and Rollins as well, but in the context of their own demandingly individual conceptions.

On Rollins' latest records, e.g., *Our Man in Jazz* (Victor

LSP-2612) and club dates, or on Coltrane's recently recorded *Live* (Impulse A-10), or in-person solos, the influence of this revived concept of free improvisation based,
finally, on the oldest sense of form in Afro-American music,
*the individual*, reaches its most impressive manifestation.
And, of course, Ornette Coleman himself, on his records, or
in person, continues to excite intrepid jazz listeners all over
the country by the fierceness and originality of his imagina-
tion. At this point in jazz the most imaginative voices continue to be saxophonists (though the pianist Cecil Taylor has
also to be cited in any list of recent innovators). And it would
seem that not only have Rollins, Coltrane and Coleman
learned from the three original saxophone innovators, Hawkins, Young and Parker, but that they themselves are seri-
ously intent on becoming innovators of the same stature. It
is certainly not a far-fetched idea.

# 1963

## A Day With Roy Haynes

IT WAS IN the Jazz Gallery, just after a young woman had come up to me and asked me whether or not I was Roy Haynes, that Roy Haynes himself took my arm and began berating me for the various faux pas and indiscretions committed on his person by that breed of noisy opportunists known as jazz critics. Part of the diatribe, I must admit, was aimed directly at me, for the various injustices that I, myself, had subjected Roy to. But I weathered the storm and at the end of it found myself invited out to Mr. Haynes' home to trade confidences. And although I accepted graciously, and perhaps too hastily, I left the Gallery with the distinct feeling that Roy didn't believe I'd show. But two days later, and four hours after the time I'd given, I was calling Roy from a pay phone asking him to pick me up at the subway station.

Roy Haynes drives a long pale yellow cadillac that looks as if it has just arrived from the plant. It gleams with the same kind of middle-class impeccability that Roy himself displays in his choice of clothes and homes and personalities. (Roy, in fact, along with Miles Davis, recently won an *Esquire* award for his sartorial elegance.) And the car, like the clothes and the home and, perhaps, the personality, is not a superfluous affectation with Haynes, it is a thing he admired and wanted, and also something he felt he deserved. Roy Haynes attitude towards his music is predictably similar. Playing jazz was something he wanted to do, and something he learned to do well, after a long apprenticeship. Recognition in his chosen field, he has found, is not as simple to get as the other things. It has been longer in coming, even though Roy feels, and quite justifiably so, that it is something he deserves.

The Haynes' home is in Hollis, Long Island. An impossible place for a jazz musician to live according to popular fiction (not to mention popular jazz sociology). It is a neat brick house with a built-in garage. It looks like the kind of house out of which each morning at 8:00 some less than intrepid American will make his dash for the 8:20 to Madison Avenue. The house is an almost indistinguishable item in the long row of neat brick homes that make up Roy Haynes' block. And yet in one of these precious middle-class structures lives one of the finest drummers in modern jazz.

The interior of the Haynes' house is as one would have expected, given the neighborhood. Recently new Danish modern (or what a friend termed "Long Island Baroque"), neat and spotless moderate-sized rooms minus the inexpensive Dufy prints his neighbors have, probably a rather bulky collection of jazz records taking up the cultural slack. While we talked, Roy kept the phonograph active (sometimes if only to emphasize a particular point by playing the music in question). Our conversation began pretty much as it had ended two nights before at the Jazz Gallery (where Roy was working with the Stan Getz quartet). Roy began by berating me mildly, in a mock conversation with his friend, for my many affronts, the most recent of which was the liner notes for an Etta Jones record.

"Now, here I've worked with one of the greatest vocalists in the business, Sarah Vaughan, for five years, and this guy doesn't mention my name once in the notes." (The friend was properly impressed and outraged.) "Wow. What's a person have to do to get some kind of notice from you critics? I'm supposed to know how to back up singers as well as anybody around, and this guy doesn't even put my name in the notes even once. How about that?"

There wasn't much I could say to that, except to protest that I thought just the mention of Roy's name among the credits was enough to let anybody who had been around jazz for any time to know that there was an excellent craftsman on the job. Roy didn't buy it. Happily the talk turned to Roy's earlier days in jazz, and his pre-New York background. Roy was born in Boston thirty-seven years ago, which is not such an advanced age for a man who can definitely be listed among the pioneers of bebop drumming. (Martin Williams has called Roy "The last of the real bebop drummers.") He studied briefly at the Boston Conservatory and then began playing around town and in Connecticut with the local big names.

"I was at Martha's Vineyard in 1945 when I got this telegram from Luis Russell asking me to come to New York. I don't know how he heard about me, because I hadn't played anywhere but in Boston and places in Connecticut. I think maybe there was a musician who was playing with Luis who heard me when he passed through Boston. Anyway, I was excited and wanted to go to New York, but I also wanted to stay up at Martha's Vineyard until I finished the gig. It was a really swinging place then, kind of a resort for really rich people. So I wrote Luis Russell and asked him could he wait until I finished the job. He wrote back telling me when and where to show up and enclosed my ticket. When I got to New York, we were opening at the Savoy."

Roy now put John Lewis' "Morpheus" on the phonograph and it sounded amazingly like the new avant-garde, even though it was made in 1950. Roy was the drummer in a group that boasted Sonny Rollins, Miles Davis, Percy Heath and Lewis, himself.

"What really turned me on to jazz was one particular record. You know that record Basie made called "The World Is Mad"? Well, that's what really got me moving. Jo Jones' solo on that tune was really out of sight. I knew right away what I wanted to do, after that.

"I quit Russell's band in 1947. Those one-nighters got to me, finally. Although, I thought it was a pretty swinging band. We had some good men. And it was the first time I had worked with a really big band. Luis had a lot of faith in me . . . I was just a young kid, a little over twenty. My brother told me something years after I'd left Russell. He said that I'd really been a big influence on the band. I mean, that the musicians started picking up on some of the things I was doing, and it changed their playing. And I was just trying to get myself together. It's a strange thing."

When "Morpheus" ended, Roy's friend suggested that he put on an album of Sarah Vaughan's.

"You know people are always asking me how it was to play with Sarah. They figure it must have been a drag, you know, playing behind a singer, and never really getting a chance to stretch out. But that's not the way it was. I thought it was a gas. Sarah's not just a singer. I mean she's fantastic, and playing with her was a ball for me. She's so great. And I always got a chance to solo. When I got tired of working with her I left. It was as simple as that. But she's a beautiful singer.

"When I started playing with Luis Russell, it was the first time I'd ever seen the South. We went through the South a lot doing all those one-nighters the band had to do. The first place we went when we left the Savoy was Maryland, which is not really the South, I guess, but it was still something else. And the rest of those tours . . . you know sometimes we played in warehouses. I remember once playing in a ware-house with a tin roof. I made a lot of southern tours with Sarah, too. Those terrible package deals. Sarah didn't dig those too much, either."

Roy has three young children and an older son by a previous marriage. All four of them made their appearances at various times, also Roy's wife.

"I left Luis Russell in 1947, and started hanging around 52nd Street. I'd already been going up to Minton's and sitting in. I learned a lot up there, too. Drummers used to have to stand in line to get a chance to play. There were so many people around who wanted to sit in, Teddy Stewart, Max (Roach), Klook (Kenny Clarke). And everybody really tried to show up good, too, every night. No matter where somebody might be working, if they were in town they'd try to make Minton's. There was a lot of good music.

"I just gigged around the street for a year, but then I went back to Russell. But I just stayed with him a year this time. When I left, I started playing with Pres. That was a really great experience. Pres could do anything. I really learned a lot being in that group, too. He always knew just the way he wanted everybody in the band to sound. I stayed with Pres for about two years. He was a really creative musician. He'd never do the same thing twice. Playing with Monk was the same, or with Bird. You never know what they'd do next. Monk was like going to school. He'd play anything and do anything."

At this point Roy put on an airshot taken from whatever radio station was broadcasting the live goings on at Birdland in 1951. Symphony Sid's baleful monotone was announcing a group that was going to play "Blue'n Boogie." The group was Charlie Parker, Dizzy Gillespie, Tommy Potter and Roy Haynes.

"It was Max's gig, but he couldn't make it. He called me up at the last minute and I got there. Listen to Bird. Sometimes you wouldn't believe the things he would do. And I sometimes wondered how I could follow him. I mean he would do anything. I was lucky to get this record. There was some guy walking around asking a fantastic price."

The group went off into "Ornithology" and another wild Parker solo.

"Yeh, I was doing just about the same things then I'm doing now. You know, I was the first drummer to work in Birdland, back in 1949. And just about that time I really got busy. 'Fifty and 'fifty-one I was always working, that was just before I went with Sarah."

The conversation shot around into a great many areas, musical and non-musical, but always there was Roy's insistence upon the shortsightedness of critics and the difficulties arising when one is trying to make a living playing jazz.

"What is it, almost seventeen years I've been around the jazz scene? You know I've never yet won any kind of poll. I haven't even ever been voted New Star or anything. And that's the only place I ever get any votes in these polls . . . as a New Star. Isn't that something? A new star, and I've been around longer than most of the old stars. I don't know what it is. And then among the critics, you know, people who are supposed to know what's happening, I still barely get mentioned. People are always saying I'm underrated . . . like it's something to be proud of. There was even a picture of me in a *Metronome* yearbook a few years back, backing up Bird, and you know what they had in the caption? They had Klook's name. If it wasn't so funny, it would really make me mad. I bet if I was some kind of nut or something, you know weird or something, I'd get a lot of notice. But there doesn't seem to be too much attention paid to guys who seem to be normal. I mean who make all their gigs and raise families. It's a wild thing."

I mentioned to Roy that I did think it was a crazy kind of situation when a musician like himself, who is really so well known and so respected by critics and musicians alike, had never won any kind of poll. Haynes is usually mentioned in any critic's or musician's list of best drummers, and judging by the frequency of his appearances with some of the younger avant-garde musicians like Eric Dolphy and Oliver Nelson, there has certainly been no lessening of Roy's gifts.

"I'll tell you a funny story about what some musicians mean when they say they respect you. I was in Chicago once, playing opposite this very well-paid group. So the drummer, whom I'd known only casually, comes over after one of our sets and tells me something like, 'Roy, you are the greatest. I've listened to you for years and really picked up so much. Man, if it wasn't for you and Max, I don't know what I'd be playing.' You know, and it was kind of nice to hear. But just a few days later I read in a magazine where this same drummer is quoted as saying his biggest influences have been Buddy Rich and Sonny Igoe. Whew, I mean, what can I say?"

During the last few minutes of talk, Roy had begun to exit and reenter the room in various stages of dress and undress, readying himself for the trip to Manhattan and his job with Stan Getz. At one point he came back into the room waving a carefully framed plaque. It was the award he had received from *Esquire* magazine for being one of the best-dressed men in show business.

"Did you see the issue of *Esquire* the award was announced in? Miles got one, too. You know this really means a lot, because I guess they must have just gotten around to giving them to Negroes. But I don't get any awards in music, my profession, just for clothes."

Roy was just about dressed, in an extremely fashionable suit that could probably bring another *Esquire* award. The record he put on for our exit, while the photographer and I were hurriedly emptying our cans of beer, was Ray Charles with Betty Carter singing "Two to Tango." Ray definitely took the tune out of the pop category; and as he hit his last note, Roy looked at his watch, made his good-byes to his family, and left.

After a few blocks Roy pulled the big car into a service station. An attendant came out and began to fiddle with the fish tails. Roy was talking about the music business, when the attendant tapped on the window. "Hey, mister, which one of these tails you open to put the gas in?"

Roy hit the electric switch sending down the window. "Man, what's the matter . . . you don't get Cadillacs in here?" He got out of the car and demonstrated.

Soon we got back on the road, Roy checking his watch every few minutes. "Well, we still have some time. I hate to be late for any gig. You know, if you're late you just don't have any excuse. You're wrong. This is a tough business in a lot of ways. I mean nobody really makes any large money. A few guys . . . people that get in magazines all the time . . . but most don't make much. Working with Sarah was what straightened me out financially. Helped me to get the house and things. But even when you're working, I mean free lance, and fairly regularly, you don't work that much. And then records are not that much. You know I just made my first date as a leader a couple of years ago. That trio album on Prestige. *We Three*. It did pretty well, too; so we followed it up with *Just Us*. But I recorded with Blue Note in nineteen hundred forty-nine and you know it was nineteen hundred fifty-nine, yeh, ten years later, before I recorded with them again. You really have to be strong."

We were coming off the bridge into Manhattan and Roy glanced at his watch again. "We made good time. I still got about five or ten minutes. You can't tell when you're following Trane. There's no telling how long that cat'll stay once he gets started. And then sometimes he plays very short sets. So I like to be fairly early."

We walked into the Gallery just as The John Coltrane Quintet was leaving the stage. Stan Getz walked into the club soon after we did, but the group didn't go up immediately because the bass player was late. I sat and talked with Roy at one of the tables, watching Getz looking nervously at his watch.

"Talking about working regularly, Stan wants me to go with him to Europe. You know he wants to work six months in Europe and six months here. But I don't know, I really don't want to leave New York for that long. It's my home, I really dig New York. I was thinking of maybe moving further out on the Island or maybe up to Connecticut. But that's still close, if you've got a car."

McCoy Tyner and Eric Dolphy came over to exchange greetings with Roy while he waited for Getz to finish shaking his finger in the bass player's face. The set began, shortly after, and Roy Haynes went to work.

After the first set Roy and I walked down the street to a delicatessen. He ordered matzo ball soup, watched the clock and answered some of my last questions. I wondered, since Roy had played with so many of the masters of modern jazz, and had been in on the music called bebop almost from the beginning, what he thought of the young innovators, many of whom he has played with already.

"Well I don't think Ornette's doing anything really new. I like some of the things he does, but a lot of people were doing the same things years ago. Oliver Nelson is a very good saxophonist, and he's written some fine things, but essentially I don't think it's anything new. There's no reason why it should have to be. Maybe he's using some different voicings or something . . . but Duke Ellington has used those way-out voicings for years.

"Young drummers? Well, there's only a couple I could pin down. So many of these young guys sound so much alike. There's one guy, Donald Bailey, who plays with Jimmy

Smith. He doesn't play many solos, but I really like what he does with the group. Also, I like Billy Higgins a lot. He thinks about drums the way I do. We've talked a lot. He doesn't play enough, though. But he's real. He plays the truth. A lot depends on conception. You've got to draw things out of drums. You can't just beat on the drums. There's much more to drumming than that. Billy knows that."

It was time to get back to his job so Roy and I left the delicatessen and got back for John Coltrane's last tune. Trane was looking up and down a scale for some note, and thrilling the audience doing it. Roy and I joined a crowd of musicians and ecstatic hippies and listened to Coltrane sing. I left Roy with a handshake when an autograph hunter came up and said, "You were playing with Stan Getz, weren't you? Will you sign this so I can have all your names here?"

# 1964

## Sonny Rollins

*Our Man in Jazz* (RCA Victor LPM-2612) Rollins, tenor; Don Cherry, cornet; Bob Cranshaw, bass; Billy Higgins, drums.
*Oleo;* "Dearly Beloved;" "Doxy" (recorded on location at The Village Gate, New York City)

IN A REVIEW I wrote of Sonny Rollins' previous Victor date, "What's New," I tried to stress that what was being recorded hadn't yet begun to approach what Rollins had been doing in person, and that when the recorded music began to sound like the in-person shots then perhaps a lot of people were going to be disturbed, one way or another. *Our Man In Jazz*, recorded live, like they say, at the Village Gate, finally begins to tell the whole story. That is, as much of it as Sonny has thus far gotten together. And he is certainly not to be stopped here at the point this record describes so wonderfully. But already, what's been accomplished is staggering.

The emotional and aesthetic balance of Sonny's new group is impeccable and so moving that at each hearing the record seems to grow in its musical profundity and excitement rather than diminish. Sonny's first Victor album, *The Bridge*, was done merely to show a hopefully expanded audience that Sonny could play pretty, which is like getting Picasso to paint post cards. He could do it, and probably quite well, but it is not really his job. The second album, *What's New*, described to some extent a few of the new areas in which Sonny's recent music had been moving, especially on the tune, "If I Would Ever Leave You." But that was done in the context of Jim Hall's lush and romantic guitar. (A lushness and romanticism that made tunes like "The Night Has a Thousand Eyes" so nearly perfect.) *Our Man* shows the move Sonny made away from the purposefully ornamental towards the harsh classicism of a music that might seem similar, in its anarchic disregard for the stale popular music of the new soul mainstream and the intent of its completely functional and organic form, like that of Ornette Coleman or the "controversial" aspect of John Coltrane. But Rollins is too singular an artist to be *similar* merely for the sake of being; he makes his moves, utilizes whatever "influences" move him, with the exacting intention of extending his own statements and providing his own music with fresh emotional stimuli. And he is certainly succeeding.

"Dearly Beloved" and "Doxy" are almost like exhaustive exercises in preparation for the long work, "Oleo," which is performed here with an intensity and imaginative concern that make estimable works like "Blues For Philly Joe" or "Wagon Wheels" or "Blue 7" or "If I Would Ever Leave You," or even "Freedom Suite," seem like art school sketches. This is a superb piece of music, and demonstrates quite impressively the "potential future" that critic Martin Williams said some time ago would be the result of Sonny's penchant for thematic improvisation. (See "Sonny Rollins and The Challenge of Thematic Improvisation," *Jazz Review*, November, 1958.) "Oleo" becomes not merely a set of chords fixed under a set of changes, but a growing and constantly changing work based on the total musical shape of the piece. In a sense the music depends for its form on the same references as primitive blues forms. It considers the *total area* of its existence as a means to evolve, i.e., to move, as an intelligently shaped musical concept, from its beginning to its end. This total area is not merely constantly stated chords, but the *more* musical considerations of rhythm, pitch, timbre and melody. All these shaped by the emotional requirements of the player, i.e., the improvising soloist (or improvising group). It becomes music "with and without occasion," in the oldest and most absolute sense of what music is. What Rollins (and Coltrane and Coleman and Cecil Taylor, and some others) have done is to reestablish the absolute hegemony of improvisation in jazz and to propose jazz again as the freest of Western music. What Busoni meant when he said, "Music was born free; and to win its freedom is its destiny."

This new group that Rollins has gotten together is right now making the most exciting in-person music in jazz. Trumpeter Don Cherry is easily the most consistently adventurous trumpet player working. The solos on "Doxy" or "Oleo" should bear this out to anyone who will listen without hoping to hear Miles Davis, Dizzy Gillespie or Louis Armstrong. This *is* new, friends.

Drummer Billy Higgins' sharp boppishly rococo attack is already patently his own, and enables the group to move where it will with the completely musical-intuitive knowledge that Higgins is preparing that place for them. His solo on "Oleo" is really fantastic (but so is the one on "Doxy"); the attack, the humor, the total rhythmic figure he provides, all work almost perfectly.

Bassist Bob Cranshaw cannot produce the excitement or astonishment the rest of the group does, but he is always heavily in evidence with a large pretty sound and constant ear that make the rest of the action possible. He is most impressive when what he is playing is the single basis for whatever improvisation is moving just above him. Then he becomes concomitantly expansive and literally sings.

*Assassins* is what I have been calling this group privately. *The Assassins.*

So now the music is here, and the "secret" completely out. I am waiting now for the "anti-jazz" people to show up with evidence that that's what Sonny's music should be called. I dare them.

# 1963

## A Jazz Great: John Coltrane

*Giant Steps* (Atlantic 1311).
*Coltrane Jazz* (Atlantic 1354). Coltrane, tenor sax; Wynton Kelly, piano; Paul Chambers, bass; Jimmy Cobb, drums. (On "Village Blues": McCoy Tyner, piano; Steve Davis, bass; Elvin Jones, drums).
"Little Old Lady," "Village Blues," "My Shining Hour," "Fifth House," "Harmonique," "Like Sonny," "I'll Wait and Pray," "Some Other Blues."
*My Favorite Things* (Atlantic 1361). Coltrane, soprano and tenor sax; McCoy Tyner, piano; Steve Davis, bass; Elvin Jones, drums.
"My Favorite Things," "Everytime We Say Goodbye," "Summertime," "But Not For Me."

WHEN AN ARTIST is termed "great" it is usually the result of one of two or maybe three distinct processes. One such process is set in motion when the artist's work so amazes and delights his peers, i.e., his fellow artists, that they are moved to immediately claim his greatness, and make so much noise about it that the professors, critics and sometimes even the public become alerted and can leap on the bandwagon before it pulls off (e.g., James Joyce, Charlie Parker). Another such process is started when the artist, even though he might be appreciated greatly by his contemporaries, is little known outside that small coterie but, nevertheless, years

later manages to be "rediscovered" either by some future
generation of artists or some intrepid scholar who happens
to be combing or "reevaluating" a particular period (e.g.,
Melville, Bunk Johnson, Ryder and maybe Lucky Thompson, unfortunately).

Still another of these means to "greatness" is that unlikely
coincidence of the artist being acclaimed great by fellow
artists, critics and the public, at the same time . . . and not
only while he is still alive, but when he is also just *beginning
to* prove that greatest concretely. John Coltrane fits this
last category, I think; in fact the general consensus was that
Coltrane was great even before he had done very much to
prove it. I remember a young vibes player telling me, "John
Coltrane is a genius," after hearing one chorus of John's solo
on "Round About Midnight," with Miles Davis six years ago.
But I think the trilogy bears out my friend's early emotive
judgment quite impressively. Coltrane is a great man (as
another friend of mine said, recently, listening to John at the
Half Note . . ."a great man.")

Actually, of course, not *all* the professors or the public are
sold on John yet. I have still heard quite reputable (even
intelligent) critics put Coltrane down for reasons that are
sometimes extra-musical, sometimes extra-rational. But to
my mind, the greatest disparagement of what John Coltrane
is doing must come from those who *cannot hear* what he is
doing. From people, well meaning and/or intelligent as they
might be, who simply do not hear the music. But another
reason why some otherwise responsible people might not be
able to hear Coltrane might be the simple fact that he is
such a singularly unclassifiable figure, in fact, almost an
*alien* power, in the presence of two distinct and almost
antagonistic camps. John's way is somewhere between the so-
called mainstream (which, fellow travelers, is *no longer* the
swing-based elder statesmen from the 30's who, still, some-

how, manage to survive, but the neo-boppers of the 50's: they are the traditionalists of this era) and those young musicians I have called the avant-garde. John Coltrane is actually in neither camp, though he is certainly a huge force in each. Most of the avant-garde reed men are beholden to John and a great many of the new mainstreamers think they are John Coltrane. Trane's influence moves in both directions . . . sometimes detrimentally (Benny Golson, Cliff Jordan, etc.) sometimes to great effect (Wayne Shorter, Archie Shepp).

Of course, Coltrane's move from being just another "hip" tenor saxophonist to the position of chief innovator on that instrument has to be traced from the beginning of his recorded efforts and all those changes, resolutions and transmutations in Coltrane's approach to his instrument and to jazz in general documented in order to get a more complete picture of just what has happened to him during the time that has intervened between that chorus with Miles and the last Atlantic album, *My Favorite Things*. And even the most confirmed Coltrane debunkers must agree that a whole lot has gone on during that time . . . like it or not. But I think the trilogy, i.e., starting with the first Atlantic album, *Giant Steps* and proceeding through the next one, *Coltrane Jazz*, and coming finally to the last one, *My Favorite Things* shows Trane's entire development, from sideman to innovator, in microcosm. Before the trilogy, and after, say, the Columbia album with Miles Davis, *Milestones* (the solo on "Straight, No Chaser"), it became increasingly evident to anyone who would listen that Coltrane was definitely moving into fresher areas of expression on his instrument. That solo, even though in some senses it was the most "lopsided," ill-thought-out solo Coltrane has produced on records, still contained more fresh thinking about how one is supposed to play the tenor saxophone post-Hawkins/Young than anyone else around had shown (with the probable exception of Sonny Rollins). The seeming masses of sixteenth notes, the *new* and finally articulated concept of using whole groups or clusters of rapidly fired notes as a chordal insistence rather than a strict melodic progression. That is, the notes that Trane was playing in the solo became more than just one note following another, in whatever placement, to make a melody. They, the notes, came so fast and with so many overtones and undertones, that they had the effect of a piano player striking chords rapidly but somehow articulating separately each note in the chord and its vibrating sub-tones. It is the prison of the changes or the recurring chords that sent Ornette Coleman and so many others recently over the hump . . . so they play as if they were paying no attention to the chords at all (which, of course, is not true). But Coltrane's reaction to the constant pounding chords and flat static, if elegant, rhythm section, was to try to play almost every note of the chord separately, as well as the related or vibrating tones that chord produced. The result, of course, is what someone termed "Sheets of Sound" or, more derogatorily, "just scales."

After "Straight, No Chaser," Trane began to find out exactly what he was doing. But a great many times the chord jungle just caused him to run around and around hoping somehow to get into that thing he'd found and was trying to work out. I heard him several times during that period, just after he'd left Monk. One night he played the head of "Confirmation" over and over again, about twenty times, and that was his solo. It was as if he wanted to take that melody apart and play out each of its chords as a separate improvisational challenge. And while it was a marvelous thing to hear and see, it was also more than a little frightening; like watching a grown man learning to speak . . . and I think that's just what was happening.

Thelonius Monk's influence on Coltrane, or at least the changes that John's playing underwent after his long employment with Monk's group at the Five Spot, cannot be stressed too much. Monk, it seemed, opened Trane's head to possibilities of rhythmic and harmonic variation that Trane had never considered before. (And it strikes me as one of the worst crimes in recent recording history that Bill Grauer didn't record any of the fantastic music Monk, Trane and Wilbur Ware were making together that summer at the Five Spot. Grauer waited until Johnny Griffin had replaced Coltrane before he sent down the tape. Oh, well . . .)

The greatest single album Coltrane made before the trilogy is, in my opinion, *Hard Driving Jazz* with Cecil Taylor. Of course, that is not to lessen the achievement or single performances, such as Trane's solos on "Soft Lights and Sweet Music," "Russian Lullaby," "Blue Trane," "Slow Dance" and so many others, but no other solos before the trilogy, with the exception of "Straight, No Chaser," are as prophetic of what was coming as Trane's solos on "Double Clutchin'" and "Shifting Down" on *Hard Driving Jazz*. In fact, the ideas that are put forth and almost articulated successfully on those two solos are not even duplicated to such a degree on the first two albums of the trilogy. "Summertime," on MFT, is the real resolution of those ideas. The long "chordal" lines and extended choruses of "Straight, No Chaser" were only the incunabula of what happens on "Shifting Down" and "Double Clutchin'." Not only are those same attacks used on these solos, but also the first real emergence of John's concern for harmonics, or at least there is some indication of what he intends to do with that long amazing chordal line.

On the album, *Coltrane Jazz*, Trane faces the harmonics problem squarely. He concentrates on it entirely, even sacrificing his characteristic "horn music" (as someone once told me . . . "John's making music on a horn . . . not a piano or a guitar or a drum, and it's a *tenor* saxophone horn, and you can see he realized it and doesn't even think it's a trumpet. Bird knew he was playing an alto saxophone, and he never tried to play it like anything else but an alto saxophone. You get into some pretty far out things when you realize just exactly what instrument *you* are playing . . .") for the sake of the tightened reed harmonic effects he wanted. "Harmonique," for strictly technical application, "Fifth House" for a more musical application. And "Fifth House," because it is a more musical application, also foreshadows John's complete triumph on "Summertime" and "But Not For Me" where the long surging chordal line seems at times to shatter into hundreds of different related notes . . . not merely horizontally, but vertically. The harmonic insistence that was stressed on *Coltrane Jazz* is suddenly integrated into that amazing line, and not only does one seem to hear each note and sub-tone of a chord being played, but also each one of those notes shattered into half and quarter tones and flying every which way.

*Giant Steps*, the first album of the trilogy, was concerned mostly with rhythmical ideas. On "Naima," "Giant Steps" and "Spiral," John seemed to be finding ways of projecting his line over entire choruses without having to restate the basic beat of the tunes. Again, this problem seems resolved marvelously on "Summertime" and "But Not For Me". . . and in the same ways he proposed on "Double Clutchin'."

The title tune of the last album of the trilogy, *My Favorite Things*, is at least a *tour de force*. But it is also, at the same time, a beginning. The use of the soprano saxophone is, of course, one reason for my terming it a beginning, but also because John seems, on his solo, to have become really interested in melody for the first time . . . i.e., he is turning his attention to that old problem in jazz of improvising on a simple and terribly strict melodic line. The repeated scale of "My Favorite Things" is so simple and final that the only means of getting out of it is to elaborate on that tender little melody. (Listen to McCoy Tyner's fantastically beautiful embroideries on that scale and melody, sometimes breaking down into almost maudlin piano exercises, sometimes hurdling two centuries to sound like rococo cocktail music, but containing as much invention and subtlety as any piano solo I've heard in the last few years . . . Monk, Cecil Taylor and John Lewis being the exceptions.) And Coltrane's use of the soprano not only springs that instrument free from the obscurity that had beset it since Sidney Bechet (Steve Lacey's valiant efforts notwithstanding), but it also opens up an entirely new mode of expression for John. The soprano, like the man said, is the soprano . . . just as the tenor is the tenor . . . and the things that can be said on each instrument are very, very different. So, if *My Favorite Things* is just the beginning of Coltrane's story on the tiny horn . . . just wait until he really learns how to play it. "Summertime" seems to me a reason for calling John Coltrane a great tenor saxophonist, and we might be able soon to call him a great soprano saxophonist. I'm sure there are a lot of people who'd be willing to do it right now, just on the basis of *My Favorite Things* . . . it's a very strong temptation for me also.

# 1964

## Coltrane Live At Birdland

*Coltrane Live at Birdland* Impulse A-50
John Coltrane, tenor and soprano saxophones
McCoy Tyner, piano
Jimmy Garrison, bass
Elvin Jones, drums

|                    (1)                    |                    (2)                    |
| ----------------------------------------- | ----------------------------------------- |
| 1. "Afro-Blue"                            | 1. "The Promise"                          |
| 2. "I Want to Talk about You"             | 2. "Alabama"                              |
|                                           | 3. "Your Lady"                            |

ONE OF THE most baffling things about America is that despite its essentially vile profile, so much beauty continues to exist here. Perhaps it's as so many thinkers have said, that it is because of the vileness, or call it adversity, that such beauty does exist. (As balance?)

Thinking along these lines, even the title of this album (A-50) can be rendered "symbolic" and more directly meaningful. *John Coltrane Live at Birdland.* To me Birdland is a

place no man should wander into unarmed, especially not an
artist, and that is what John Coltrane is. But, too, Birdland is
only America in microcosm, and we know how high the
mortality rate is for artists in this instant tomb. Yet, the title
tells us that John Coltrane is there *live*. In this tiny America
where the most delirious happiness can only be caused by
the dollar, a man continues to make daring reference to some
other kind of thought. Impossible? Listen to "I Want to Talk
about You."

Coltrane apparently doesn't need an ivory tower. Now
that he is a master, and the slightest sound from his instrument is valuable, he is able, literally, to make his statements
anywhere. Birdland included. It does not seem to matter to
him (nor should it) that hovering in the background are
people and artifacts that have no more to do with his music
than silence.

But now I forget why I went off into this direction. Nightclubs are, finally, nightclubs. And their value is that even
though they are raised or opened strictly for gain (and not
the musician's) if we go there and are able to sit, as I was
for this session, and hold on, if it is a master we are listening
to, we are very likely to be moved beyond the pettiness and
stupidity of our beautiful enemies. John Coltrane can do this
for us. He has done it for me many times, and his music is
one of the reasons suicide seems so boring.

There are three numbers on the album that were recorded
*Live* at Birdland, "Afro-Blue," "I Want to Talk about You"
and "The Promise." And while some of the nonmusical hys-
teria has vanished from the recording, that is, after riding a
subway through New York's bowels, and that subway full of
all the things any man should expect to find in something's
bowels, and then coming up stairs to the street and walking
slowly, head down, through the traffic and failure that does
shape this place, and then entering "The Jazz Corner Of The
World," a temple erected in praise of what God (?), and

then finally amidst that noise and glare to hear a man destroy all of it, completely, like Sodom, with just the first few
notes from his horn, your "critical" sense can be erased completely, and that experience can place you somewhere a long
way off from anything ugly. Still, what was of musical value
that I heard that night does remain, and the emotions . . .
some of them completely new . . . that I experience at each
"objective" rehearing of this music are as valuable as anything else I know about. And all of this *is* on this record, and
the studio pieces, "Alabama" and "Your Lady" are among the
strongest efforts on the album.

But since records, recorded "live" or otherwise, are artifacts, that is the way they should be talked about. The few
people who were at Birdland the night of October 8, or
rather, the fewer people there that night, who really *heard*
what Coltrane, Jones, Tyner and Garrison were doing will
probably tell you, if you ever run into them, just exactly
what went on, and how we all reacted. I wish I had a list of
all those people so that interested parties could call them
and get the whole story, but then, almost anyone who's
heard John and the others at a nightclub or some kind of live
performance, has got stories of their own. I know I've got a
lot of them.

But in terms of the artifact, what you're holding in your
hand now, I would say first of all, if you can hear, you're
going to be moved. "Afro-Blue, " the long tune of the album,
is in the tradition of all the African-Indian-Latin flavored
pieces Trane has done on soprano, since picking up that
horn and reclaiming it as a jazz instrument. (In this sense
"The Promise" is in that same genre.) Even though the head-
melody is simple and songlike, it is a song given by making
what feels to me like an almost unintelligible lyricism suddenly and marvelously intelligible. McCoy Tyner, too, who
is the polished formalist of the group, makes his own less
cautious lyrical statements on this, but driven, almost

harassed, as Trane is, too, by the mad ritual drama that
Elvin Jones taunts them with. There is no way to describe
Elvin's playing or, I would suppose, Elvin himself. The long
tag of "Afro-Blue," with Elvin thrashing and cursing beneath
Trane's line is unbelievable. Beautiful has nothing to do with
it, but it is. (I got up and danced while writing these notes,
screaming at Elvin to cool it.) You feel when this is finished,
amidst the crashing cymbals, bombarded tom-toms, and
above it all Coltrane's soprano singing like any song you can
remember, that it really did not have to end at all, that this
music could have gone on and on like the wild pulse of all
living.

Trane did Billy Eckstine's "I Want to Talk about You"
some years ago, but I don't think it's any news that his style
has changed a great deal since then, and so this "talk" is
something completely different. It is now a virtuoso tenor
piece (and the tenor is still Trane's real instrument) and
instead of the simplistic though touching note-for-note re-
play of the ballad's line, on this performance each note is
tested, given a slight tremolo or emotional vibrato (note to
chord to scale reference), which makes it seem as if each
one of the notes is given the possibility of "infinite" qualifica-
tion, i.e., scalar or chordal expansion . . . threatening us with
those "sheets of sound," but also proving that the ballad as it
was written was only the beginning of the story. The tag on
this is an unaccompanied solo of Trane's that is a tenor
lesson-performance that seems to get more precisely stated
with each rehearing.

If you have heard "Slow Dance" or "After the Rain," then
you might be prepared for the kind of feeling that "Alabama" carries. I didn't realize until now what a beautiful
word *Alabama* is. That is one function of art, to reveal
beauty, common or uncommon, uncommonly. And that's
what Trane does. Bob Thiele asked Trane if the title, "had
any significance to today's problems." I suppose he meant

literally. Coltrane answered, "It represents, musically, something that I saw down there translate~ ~nto music from inside me." Which is to say, "listen." And what we're given is a slow delicate introspective sadness, almost hopelessness, except for Elvin, rising in the background like something out of nature . . . a fattening thunder . . . storm clouds or jungle war clouds. The whole is a frightening emotional portrait of some place, in these musicians' feelings. If that "real" Alabama was the catalyst, more power to it, and may it be this beautiful, even in its destruction.

"Your Lady" is the sweetest song on the date. And it is pure song, say, as an accompaniment for some very elegant uptown song and dance man. Elvin Jones' heavy tingling parallel counterpoint sweeps the line along, and the way he is able to solo constantly beneath Trane's flights, commenting, extending or just going off on his own, is a very important part of the total sound and effect of this Coltrane group. Jimmy Garrison's constancy, and power, which must be fantastic to support, stimulate and push this group of powerful (and diverse) personalities, is already almost legendary. On tunes like "Lady" or "Afro-Blue," Garrison's bass booms so symmetrically and steadily and emotionally and, again, with such strength, that one would guess that he must be able to tear safes open with his fingers.

All the music on this album is *live*, whether it was recorded above the drunks and clowns at Birdland, or in the studio. There is a daringly human quality to John Coltrane's music that makes itself felt, wherever he records. If you can hear, this music will make you think of a lot of weird and wonderful things. You might even become one of them.

*Notes on Recent Performance: 1964*

In a review of *Lush Life* which appeared in *The Urbanite*, I warned that if John Coltrane ever started to play *his own* music a whole bunch of people would be frightened out of their wits. I based that statement not so much on Trane's recorded efforts (although the solos on *Hard Drivin' Jazz* did alert me to what the future Coltrane might sound like) but on the basis of his fantastic live performances. Almost immediately after this review appeared Atlantic issued the *Coltrane Jazz* LP, and it bore out some of my warning, quite impressively. Then, of course, came the *My Favorite Things* album and a musical coup. But at a rather extended engagement at the Village Gate (alias, The Cave Of The Winds), again, Coltrane's performances outstripped anything heard on his records.

Not only has Trane gone ahead developing the long chordal line, but his use of harmonics, especially on the small horn, seems nearing perfection. On some of the soprano solos Coltrane begins one of his long lines and without decreasing the power or drive of the solo the line suddenly seems to spread itself into two or three separate lines. It is Trane's mastery of the harmonics first demonstrated on *Coltrane Jazz* and brought to such good account on *My Favorite Things* taken even further. At times one is not certain which of the notes he's hearing is, in fact, the real note, or which line the real line, i.e., the one that would be called for on a chart. Also, the rest of the group, especially Elvin Jones and McCoy Tyner can scare you to death.

There seems no doubt in my mind now that John Coltrane is the most impressive voice on the tenor saxophone of our times. And I say this with only a hesitant look over my shoulder in the direction of the Jazz Gallery where it is rumored that the old man of the mountain, Sonny Rollins, will soon reappear. (And if we get Sonny, Trane and Ornette Coleman working at the same time, I want people to stop telling me how hip Paris is!)

# 1961

## The Jazz Avant-Garde

THERE IS DEFINITELY an avant-garde in jazz today. A burgeoning group of young men who are beginning to utilize not only the most important ideas in "formal" contemporary music, but more important, young musicians who have started to utilize the most important ideas contained in that startling music called bebop. (Of course I realize that to some of my learned colleagues almost anything that came after 1940 is bebop, but that's not exactly what I meant.) And I think this last idea, the use of bop, is the most significant aspect of the particular avant-garde I'm referring to, since almost any so-called modern musicians can tell you all about Stravinsky, Schoenberg, Bartok, etc., or at least they think they can. I say *particular* avant-garde since I realize that there is also another so-called "new music," called by some of my more serious colleagues, *Third Stream*, which seeks to invest jazz with as much "classical" music as blatantly as possible. But for jazzmen now to have come to the beautiful and logical conclusion that bebop was perhaps the most legitimately complex, emotionally rich music to come out of this country, is, for me, a brilliant beginning for a "new" music.

Bebop is roots, now, just as much as blues is. "Classical" music is not. But "classical" music, and I mean now contemporary Euro-American "art" music, might seem to the

black man isolated, trying to exist within white culture
(arty or whatever), like it should be "milked" for as
many *definitions* as possible, i.e., *solutions* to engineering
problems the contemporary jazz musician's life is sure
to raise. I mean, more simply, Ornette Coleman has
had to live with the attitudes responsible for Anton
Webern's music whether he knows that music or not.
They were handed to him along with the whole history of
formal Western music, and the musics that have come to
characterize the Negro in the United States came to exist as
they do today only through the acculturation of this entire
history. And actually knowing that history, and trying
to relate to it culturally, or those formal Euro-American
musics, only adds to the *indoctrination*. But jazz and blues
*are* Western musics; products of an Afro-American culture.
But the definitions must be black no matter the geography
for the highest meaning to black men. And in this sense
European anything is irrelevant.

We are, all of us, *moderns*, whether we like it or not.
Trumpet player Ruby Braff is *responsible*, finally, to the
same ideas and attitudes that have shaped our world as
Ornette Coleman. (Ideas are things that must drench everyone, whether directly or obliquely). The same history has
elapsed in the world for both of them, and what has gone
before has settled on both of them just as surely as if they
were the same man. For Ornette Coleman, as it was for
Charlie Parker *or* James Joyce, the relationship between
their actual lives and their work seems direct. For Braff or
for Charlie Parker and Bud Powell imitators or Senator
Goldwater, the relationship, the meaning, of all the ideas
that history has stacked so wearily in front of them, and
some utilization in their own lives, is less direct. But if an
atomic bomb is dropped on Manhattan, moldy figs will die
as well as modernists, and just because some cornet player
looks out his window and says "what's going on" does not

mean that he will not be in on things. He goes, too. (I am trying to explain "avant-garde." Men for whom history exists to be *utilized* in their lives, their art, to make something for themselves and not as an overpowering reminder that people and their ideas did live before us.) "How to play exactly what I feel," is what one of these musicians told me. How? (Which is a *technical* consideration.)

Before I go further, I want to explain *technical* so as not to be confused with people who think that Thelonius Monk is "a fine pianist, but limited technically." But by *technical*, I mean more specifically being able to use what important ideas are contained in the residue of history or in the now-swell of living. For instance, to be able to doubletime Liszt piano pieces might help one to become a musician, but it will not make a man aware of the fact that Monk was a greater composer than Liszt. And it is the consciousness, on whatever level, of facts, ideas, etc., like this that are *the* most important part of technique. Knowing how to play an instrument is the barest superficiality if one is thinking of becoming a musician. It is the ideas that one utilizes *instinctively* that determine the degree of profundity any artist reaches. To know, in some way, that it is better to pay attention to Duke Ellington than to Aaron Copland is part of it. (And it is exactly because someone like Oscar Peterson has instinctive profundity that technique *is* glibness. That he can play the piano rather handily just makes him easier to identify. There is no serious instinct working at all.)

To my mind, *technique* is inseparable from what is finally played as content. A *bad* solo, no matter how "well" it is played is still *bad*.

APHORISMS: "Form can never be more than an extension of content." (Robert Creely) "Form is determined by the nature of matter. . . . Rightly viewed, order is nothing objective;

it exists only relatively to the mind." (Psalidas) "No one who can finally be said to be a 'mediocre' musician can be said to possess any *technique*." (Jones)

"Formal" music, for the jazz musician, should be *ideas*. Ideas that can make it easier for this modern jazz player to get at his roots. And as I have said, the strongest of these roots are blues and what was called bebop. They sit autonomous. Blues and bebop are *musics*. They are understandable, emotionally, as they sit: without the barest discussion of their origins. And the reason I think for this is that they *are* origins, themselves. Blues is a beginning. Bebop, a beginning. They define other varieties of music that come after them. If a man had not heard blues, there is no reason to assume that he would be even slightly interested in, say, Joe Oliver (except perhaps as a curio or from some obscure social conviction). Cannonball Adderley is *only* interesting because of bebop. And not because he plays bebop, but because he will occasionally repeat an idea that bop once represented as profound. An idea that we love, no matter what the subsequent disfigurement.

The *roots*, blues and bop, are emotion. The *technique*, the ideas, the way of handling the emotion. And this does not leave out the consideration that certainly there is pure intellect that can come out of the emotional experience and the rawest emotions that can proceed from the ideal apprehension of any hypothesis. The point is that such displacement must exist as instinct.

To go further towards a general delineation of the musicians I will cite later as part of a growing jazz avant-garde, I think first I should furnish at least two more definitions, or distinctions.

Using, or implementing an idea or concept is not necessarily imitation and, of course, the converse is true; imitation is not necessarily use. I will say first that use is proper, as well as *basic*. Use means that some idea or system is employed, but in order to reach or understand quite separate and/or dissimilar systems. Imitation means simply reproduction (of a concept), for its own sake. Someone who sings exactly like Billie Holiday or someone who plays exactly like Charlie Parker (or as close as they can manage) *produces* nothing. Essentially, there is nothing added to the universe. It is as if these performers stood on a stage and did nothing at all. Ornette Coleman uses Parker only as a hypothesis; his (Coleman's) conclusions are quite separate and unique. Sonny Rollins has certainly listened quite a bit to Gene Ammons, but Rollins' conclusions are insistently his own, and are certainly more profound than Ammons'. A man who rides the IND to work doesn't necessarily have to think he's a subway. (And a man who thinks he's a subway is usually just crazy. It will not help him get to work either.)

REEDS: *Ornette Coleman, Eric Dolphy*, Wayne Shorter, Oliver Nelson, Archie Shepp.

BRASS: *Don Cherry, Freddie Hubbard.*

PERCUSSION: *Billy Higgins, Ed Blackwell*, Dennis Charles (drums); Earl Griffith (vibraharp).

BASS: *Wilbur Ware, Charlie Haden*, Scott LaFaro, Buell Neidlinger, others.

PIANO: *Cecil Taylor.*

COMPOSITION: *Ornette Coleman, Eric Dolphy, Wayne Shorter*, Cecil Taylor.*

These are most of the people this essay intends to hamper with the *nom de guerre* avant-garde. (There are a few others like Ken McIntyre whom I think, from the reports I've received, also belong in the group, but I've not yet had a chance to listen.) The names in italics are intended to serve as further delineation as far as the quality and quantity of

* See note at end of essay.

these players' innovations. Hence, Ornette Coleman sits by himself in the reeds, Dolphy in his groove and Shorter, Nelson and Shepp in theirs. (There are more bass players than anything else simply because the chief innovator on that instrument, Wilbur Ware, has been around longer and more people have had a chance to pick up.)

But actually, this naming of names is not meant as a strict categorizing of "styles." Each of these men has his *own* way of playing, but as a group they represent, at least to me, a definite line of departure.

Melodically and rhythmically each of these players use bebop extensively. Coleman's "Ramblin' " possesses a melodic line the spatial tensions of which seem firmly rooted in 1940's Gillespie-Parker composition and extemporization. The very jaggedness and abruptness of the melodic fabric itself suggest the boppers' seemingly endless need for deliberate and agitated rhythmical contrast, most of the melodies being almost extensions of the dominating rhythmical patterns. Whistle "Ramblin'," then any early Monk, e.g., "Four in One" or "Humph" or Bird's "Cheryl" or "Confirmation," and the basic *physical* similarities of melodic lines should be immediately apparent. There seems to be an endless changing of direction; stops and starts; variations of impetus; a "jaggedness" that reaches out of the rhythmic bases of the music. (It seems to me that only Jackie McLean of the post-bop "traditionalists" has as much linear contrast and rhythmic modulation in his compositions and playing as the boppers, e.g., "Dr. Jackle," "Condition Blue," etc.) In fact, in bop and avant-garde compositions it seems as if the rhythmic portion of the music is inserted directly into the melodic portion. The melody of *Ramblin'* is almost a rhythmic pattern itself. Its accents are almost identical to the rhythmic underpinnings of the music. The same was true in bop. The very name bebop comes from an onomatopoetic attempt to reproduce the new rhythms that had engendered this music, hence; *bebop*, and with that rebop. (While it is true that "scat" singing came into use in the early days of jazz, "bopping," the kind of scat singing (scatting) that became popular during the 40's was more intent on reproducing rhythmic effects and as such making a melody out of them, e.g., *OoShubeeDobee Oo Oo* or *OoBopsh'bam-a-keukumop*, etc. But even in the incunabula of jazz and blues, something like the chants and field hollers were little more than highly rhythmical lyrics.)

One result of this "insertion" of rhythm into the melodic fabric of bop as well as the music of the avant-garde is the subsequent freedom allowed to instruments that are normally supposed to carry the entire rhythmic impetus of the music. Drum and bass lines are literally "sprung" . . . away from the simple, cloying 4/4 that characterized the musics that came immediately before and after bop. And while it is true that the post-boppers took their impetus from bop, I think the development of the *cool school* served to obscure the really valuable legacies of bop. Rhythmic diversity and freedom were the really valuable legacies. The cool tended to regularize the rhythms and make the melodic line smoother, less "jagged," relying more on "formal" variation of the line in the strict theme and variation sense. More and more emphasis was put on "charts" and written parts. Formal European music began to be canonized not only as a means but as some kind of *model*. The insistence of Brubeck, Shorty Rogers, Mulligan, John Lewis, that they could write fugues and rondoes or even improvise them was one instance. The almost legitimate harmonies that were used in cool or West Coast jazz reminded one of the part singing tradition of Europe. And groups like Shorty Rogers' Giants made a music that sounded like it came out of an organ grinder, the variations and improvisations as regular and static as a piano roll.

The "hard boppers" sought to revitalize jazz, but they did not go far enough. Somehow, they had lost sight of the important items to be gotten from bop and substituted largeness of timbre and the recent insistence on quasi-gospel influences for actual rhythmic diversity. The usual rhythms of the post-cool hard bopper of the 50's are amazingly static and smooth compared to the jazz of the 40's and the 60's. The rhythmic freedom of the 40's is lost in the 50's only to be rediscovered in the 60's. Because rhythm and melody complement each other so closely in the "new" music, both bass player and drummer also can play "melodically." They need no longer to be strictly concerned with thumping along, merely carrying the beat. The melody itself contains enough rhythmic accent to propel and stabilize the horizontal movement of the music, giving both direction and impetus. The rhythm instruments can then serve to elaborate on the melody itself. Wilbur Ware's playing is a perfect example of this. And so it is that drummers like Blackwell, Higgins and Charles can roam around the melody, giving accent here, inferring actual melody elsewhere. Elvin Jones, in his recent work with John Coltrane, also shows that he understands the difference between playing melody and "elegant" elaboration around a static rhythm.

So if the heavily accented melody springs the rhythm section, it also gives the other soloists more room to swing. The strict 4/4 is missing, and the horn men can even improvise on the melodic efforts of the rhythm section. This is one reason why in a group like Coleman's it seems as if they have gone back to the concept of collective improvisations. No one's role in the group is as *fixed* as it was in the "part singers" of the 50's. Everyone has a chance to play melody or rhythm. Cecil Taylor's left hand is used as much as a purely rhythmic insistence as it is for the melodic-harmonic placement of chords. The left hand constantly varies the rhythms his music is hinged on. Both Taylor and Coleman constantly utilize melodic variations based on rhythmic figures. Bebop proved that so called "changes," i.e., the repeated occurrence of certain chords basic to the melodic and harmonic structure of a tune, are almost arbitrary. That is, that they need not be *stated*, and that since certain chords infer certain improvisatory uses of them, why not improvise on what the chords infer rather than playing the inference itself.

The greater part of the avant-garde's contribution is melodic and rhythmic; only a few have made any notable moves harmonically, though Coleman and Dolphy tend to utilize certain ideas that are also in use in contemporary "European" music, notably, timbre as a harmonic principle. That is, where the actual sound of the horn, regardless of the note, contributes *unmeasured* harmonic diversity. (Also check out the hard blues singer, as a *first*. John Coltrane has done some marvelous work in harmonics as well.) Nelson, Shepp and Shorter also, to a lesser degree, utilize this concept, and even stranger, Shorter and Nelson have learned to utilize the so called "honking" sounds of the rhythm and blues bands to great effect. Nothing was wrong with honking in the first place, except that most of the R&B people who honked did little else.

It is also important that all of the reed players I have named are intrigued by the sound of the human voice. And it is my idea that jazz cannot be removed too far from the voice, since the whole concept of Afro-American music is hinged on vocal references. Earlier, I mentioned my belief that bebop and blues are almost autonomous musics. To add some weight, or at least provide a measure of clarification, I'd add that not only are blues and bebop the two facets of Afro-American music that utilize the rhythmic potentials of the music most directly, but also they are the two musics in which the vocal traditions of African music are most apparent. Purely instrumental blues is still the closest western instruments can come to sounding like the human voice, and the horns of Charlie Parker, Sonny Rollins, John Coltrane and most of the reed players of the new avant-garde maintain this tradition as well. The timbres of these horns suggest the human voice much more than the "legitimate", i.e., white, instrumental sound of swing or the staid, relatively cool timbres that were in evidence post-bop.

I mention these general aspects of what I have termed the avant-garde, i.e., their rhythmic and melodic concepts and the use of timbral effects to evoke the vocal beginnings of jazz, but only to show a line of demarcation. There are certainly a great many "new" features individual players possess that are not common to the group as a whole, individual discoveries and/or idiosyncracies that give each player his easily identifiable style. To name a few: the unusual harmonies that Wayne Shorter employs in his writing and his integration of Rollins' use of space and John Coltrane's disdain for it; (Shorter's main trouble, it now seems, is The Jazz Messengers.) Vibist Earl Griffith's lovely discovery that one can play the vibes like Lester Young, instead of continuing to imitate Milt Jackson's appropriation of Coleman Hawkins; Griffith's light, gauzy tone and behind-the-beat placement of his line all point to Pres and a fresh approach to vibes. Charlie Haden's guitar player approach to the bass, even going as far, sometimes, as *strumming* the big instrument; Don Cherry's fantastic melodic sense (I think that Cherry is the only *real* innovator on his instrument). Archie Shepp's refusal to admit most of the time that there is a melody or Oliver Nelson's use of R&B and so called "Mickey Mouse" timbres to beautiful effect. All these are separate facets of this new music, an amassing of talent and ideas that indicate a fresh road for jazz.

The first music Negroes made in this country had to be African; its subsequent transmutation into what we know as blues and the parallel development of jazz demonstrated the amazing flexibility of the basic character of the music. But to move as far away from the parent music as popular swing, or so-called West Coast jazz, or even into the artificially exciting, comparatively staid regular rhythms of hard-bop traditionalism demonstrates how the African elements of the music can be rendered almost to neutrality. Blues was the initial Afro-American music, and bebop the reemphasis of the non-western tradition. And if the latter saved us from the vapid wastes of swing, singlehandedly, the new avant-garde (and John Coltrane) are saving us from the comparatively vapid 50's. And they both utilized the same general methods: getting the music back to its initial rhythmic impetuses and away from the attempts at rhythmic regularity and melodic predictability that the 30's and the 50's had laid on it.

*Note: This was a picture of a newly forming avant-garde, 1961 or thereabouts. For the most part, it proved accurate, but some of the musicians listed were given more credit, than their later performances, lives, etc. have proved out, usually because at the time they were moving under the influence of some of the real innovators and movers. Some of this list have, already, either died (Scott LaFaro, one of Ornette's many white bassists, Earl Griffith, a really fantastic vibes player, who got there way before Bobby Hutcherson . . . and of course Eric Dolphy, one of the grimmest musical losses of this grim little age) or dropped out of the jazz thing for other things—Buell Neidlinger, to work in a symphony orchestra; when the piece was written he was working with Cecil Taylor. When you ask about a white musician once prominent in jazz, "Well, what ever happened to . . ." chances are he's gone back to European music, in one capacity or another, viz, Neidlinger and Don Ellis (and for these two there are many many more) or into the lucrative studio gigs, television, radio, movies, (and music executive bigs like*

*Director of Music of the Play Boy Clubs or of MGM) that have never really opened to black musicians. Others like Wilbur Ware had dues to pay that were just too strong, or like Oliver Nelson, occasionally, they have taken their talents and gone on over to Marlboro Country, where all dee big dough is.*

# 1959

## Introducing Wayne Shorter

I KNEW Wayne Shorter first in Newark where we were both, malevolently, born. He was one of the two "weird" Shorter brothers that people mentioned occasionally, usually as a metaphorical reference, ". . . as weird as Wayne." Wayne and I never ran together, or got on very intimate terms; we lived in distant parts of the city, went to different schools.

Wayne went to Newark's Arts High School. I used to see him in the too-tight green and gray band uniform, tooting on a silver horn. Or meet him on High Street always "clean," rather distant and smiling, what I've come to know as a really "secret" smile. He was playing tenor with a young group at most of the high school crowd's dances throughout the city. The band was Nat Phipps', and I wish some one had recorded them. All fifteen, sixteen, seventeen, they played, then, with a mature musicianship that would, I'm afraid, make the Farmingdale High School band sound dreary. (The Phipps band, by the way, still plays around Newark, and still has several very good musicians.)

Wayne was precocious; I heard many pretty astounding things he was doing at seventeen and eighteen. Even then, when he couldn't do anything else, he could still make you gasp at sheer technical infallibility. That was when almost every young body playing any kind of an instrument, even bongo players, sounded like Charlie Parker. Wayne did, too. But even as a Bird lover in a high school band, Wayne managed to come up with power. I remember telling somebody, "Well, that's the hippest imitation of Parker you'll ever hear." Nowadays, Charlie Parker's got nothing to do with Wayne, except, perhaps, in the sense that Bird is an "influence" on all black jazz.

When I got out of Newark permanently, after college, I heard about Wayne occasionally. Usually, talking over old times with old cronies just out of their teens and mentioning, almost wet-eyed, "You remember how Wayne Shorter used to play those fantastic solos at the Masonic Temple?", tapping on the table in a tempo so fast, Wayne would probably still have trouble making it. But that's a sense of it; the kind of aura he cast even as an adolescent, maybe because we were all adolescents . . . but I think not. I think Wayne carries that aura around him like an expensive Chesterfield. Talking to him one senses immediately this air of "invincibility." Hearing him play, one is convinced it is no mere air.

Wayne went to N.Y.U. and graduated with a degree in Music Education. But all during this time, he was still playing with the Phipps band, and staying over in New York playing at sessions with the bigtimers. It was at one of these sessions that he met John Coltrane, and they became very close friends. It was also during this time that Coltrane had just gone with Miles Davis. John talked and played, Wayne listened and also played.

After school, Wayne played around for a while and then, due largely to a session he was in at a Newark spot called Sugar Hill, was taken into the Horace Silver group. Wayne made a few dates with them, including Birdland and Newport in 1956, but then the Army got him. Luckily, he managed to get into the Fort Dix band and stay there. He came to New York every weekend, making sessions and getting heard. He got out of the Army late last year, and in his brother Allen's words, "Man, he went to the Army and took care of a lot of business." Wayne started writing, practiced a lot and, most of all, came out of it his own man, playing his horn like *nobody else* around. He had passed through two very critical stages of his life: the young precocious imitator of Bird, and the "good" young session musician whose ideas have not quite jelled. He is, now, almost at that third even more critical stage of his career: the Innovator. He still has a little way to go, but not so much as to make anyone who's heard him recently doubt for a second that he'll make it.

I'd say Wayne's style is linked to the two major tenor saxophonists of our day: Sonny Rollins and John Coltrane. From Rollins, he has learned what proper utilization of "space" (rests, doubletimes, "running through" bar lines, etc.) can do in improvisation. Like Rollins', his solos are orderly and precise, but, watching Wayne play, both eyes tight shut and smiling during his short breaks, it is obvious that the only chart he uses is somewhere behind his eyes. But Rollins seems to stand, like Joyce, above and beyond his work, paring his nails, Wayne and Coltrane are right in the middle of the music, broiling up at you with what seems to be a fantastic emotional thrust but never railing or waving their arms meaninglessly.

But Wayne's music (the playing, the compositions) is unique and seems, above all, important. The playing is characterized by an almost "literary" (in the best sense of the word) arrangement of musical relationships. Everything that comes out of the horn seems not only "premeditated" (the fire and surprise of instantaneous extemporization is always present), but definite and assimilated . . . no matter how wild or unlikely it might sound at first. He seems to be willing to try anything. He usually makes it.

When I started this piece, Wayne was playing tenor with Maynard Ferguson's big band, but since he has gone into Art

Blakey's Messengers. The night I went up to see Wayne with the Fergusons I talked to Wayne after each of three sets, wanting to get his voice in this article:

"Well, of course, you don't get as many solos as you'd like, but a lot of times things happen in a small group, and besides we've got a few people in this thing who really cook. Slide Hampton, the trombone player, he writes some fine things. We'll probably play some of Slide's things later. You know, I've got a few tunes in the book, too. . . .

"What it comes to is seriousness! Nothing comes to anything unless you're serious about it. Man, that's the only things I dig . . . serious people doing serious things . . . otherwise, there's not much to it. Of course, there's such a thing as serious humor, too. You know? Like Monk. Man, that cat's jokes are dead serious! To me, that's what people like Sonny and John represent, a really serious approach to music. And with people that are constantly improvising, you can see the real accomplishment. It's amazing! At least, it amazes me. John especially. I mean, he doesn't ever stop taking care of business."

"What about traditional jazz musicians? Have you ever listened to Jelly Roll Morton or Louis or early Duke, with a conscious desire to incorporate their approaches?"

"Well, no. Although I've listened to a lot of traditional people, especially Louis and Duke, and may have gotten a couple of things they were doing, unconsciously, but I can just about feel what they were doing without having to play that way myself to find out. You know, what Bird played came right through, and from everybody. Everybody who's saying anything plays like they've heard everybody. I'd like to make a record of Monk tunes, and one of Tad Dameron's tunes. Of course, Monk's are greater, but Tad did a lot of things that help all composers out. But, Monk, whew!"

"Well, if you do a record of Monk's tunes, I wish you'd do some of those great things nobody does because they're so tough to do, 'Four-In-One,' 'Humph,' things like that."

"You said it, man. Everybody's afraid of those tunes." He laughed, "I don't blame 'em either.

"You know, when you're into something . . . like John, you may make a lot of fluffs and clinkers . . . but that's in it, too. All that stuff counts. If you're really doing something, you can't be safe . . . you've just got to blow . . . and try to take care of some kind of business (smiles) some way. Gee, I hope we play those tunes of Slide's and mine this set. I feel like playing something."

"Does Maynard take requests?"

"Yeh, sure . . . he goes for that. You know, like you're a fan!"

"O.K., what tunes shall I ask for?"

"Well, the best of Slide's tunes is called 'Newport;' mine is 'Nellie Bly.' "

After "Oleo," the band went off into Slide Hampton's "Newport," swinging, lush, brassy. Halfway through the tune, Wayne got up to solo; after his first few notes, it was apparent to almost everyone in Birdland that the young man playing was the most exciting thing that had happened all night. The only thing wrong with the solo was that it was too short. Taken at a seemingly impossible double-timed tempo, it still was full of the kind of fierce, certainly satirical, humor that characterizes a Monk or a Rollins. When Wayne finished the solo, most of the Birdland patrons broke into a loud happy applause. The minute the band went into Wayne's "Nellie Bly," a thirties hipster-type behind me called out excitedly, "Oh, oh . . . some of that uptown stuff." He started popping his fingers vociferously. Wayne's solo, this time, was even better. Half the solo at double-time tempo. The fellows in the band broke up. The coda was supposed to be a unison thing with Wayne and Ferguson, but Ferguson fluffed so badly, Wayne reared back on his haunches and blew a long, long, sustained, Ammons-like "honk," throughout the entire passage. The old timer in back of me fell out of his chair.

I walked towards the subway with the old man in pursuit. "You know," he said, "You can tell the bosses right away and that boy's sure one of 'em."

I agreed happily and he shook my hand warmly as we parted, taking "A" trains north and south.

*Note: Wayne Shorter went on since this article to become a "star sideman" in groups as illustrious as Art Blakey's Jazz Messengers and The Miles Davis Quintet, in which he still plays. However, he has never really "stretched out" as far as his early promise seemed to demand. I still think that in 1959, Wayne was playing as tough as Coltrane, but perhaps the weight of those two steady gigs (with Blakey and Miles) boxed him in more than health called for.*               LJ

# 1963

## Introducing: Dennis Charles

DENNIS LIVES in a four-flight walkup on 118th Street between Fifth and Lenox. (Near the heart of the dope country.) When I got there, around two P.M., about an hour late, he had just gotten out of bed, "A few seconds before."

Dennis Charles was born in St. Croix, V.I. in 1937, and has been in the United States since 1945. His father is still in St. Croix, but his mother left there, after separation, and came to New York. Dennis was raised in Harlem with two brothers. His younger brother, Frank, also plays drums. And on many weekends Frank and Dennis get together working out with calypso bands; both brothers play the conga as well as a regular set.

Dennis started drumming in 1954. He studied in New York Vocational School, and he also played the conga when he was still in the West Indies. His father and grandfather also played the conga. (And I suppose most everybody else down there.)

At seventeen, which seems a right age for most any black boy, he got into trouble with the law. They took him off the streets for two years. When he got back the first thing he remembers, according to him, is Blakey's "Tempus Fugit." "Blakey's playing on that side really touched me." He goes on, "I was messed up then . . . I didn't know any better. Especially in this environment . . . coming from the West

Indies . . . where I was down there living like nature boy.

"Social workers used to come down here and hang out with us. Took us to movies . . . gave parties and invited other gangs . . . and before you knew it they'd broken all that stuff up. But that's why I got into trouble around here, because there's nothing to do.

"I didn't get a drum set until Buell (Neidlinger) bought me one when we were opening at the Five Spot around 1957. I used my brother's drums until then. When I first started to learn . . . after about four months with my brother's drums . . . I used to listen to Art and try to imitate what he was doing. I used to listen though, like a bitch. Bird records! Everybody used to listen to Bird and Monk and Blakey.

"It was much different then . . . there was no rock and roll then. Was a lot of block parties . . . a much hipper scene then, people applejacking. Except for the gangbusters. All those guys are junkies . . . used to be around here gangbusting, killing each other, now they're strung out, hanging out, high.

"I played with a calypso group at the Blue Room on 126th Street. Calypso, ChaCha . . . one night, Fridays. But I was still listening. I didn't have any jazz things under control. I could play calypso with my eyes closed. But I was always a jazz freak. And the calypso gig was good, because I learned all kinds of rhythms.

"After I started getting halfway together I used to go up to Connie's. I met Cecil (Taylor) and he asked me to come down to his house. I met Buell, Steve Lacey and that's when I really started. I used to go down there to practice. I had one snare drum.

"I told Buell before the Five Spot job that I couldn't work because I didn't have any drums. And he told me not to worry about it. The next day he took me up to the drum shop and bought me another set of drums. Funny thing is that they got stolen when we were still at the Five Spot. I lost money on the deal because the man at the drum shop gave me a phoney price on the new set, and Joe Termini (owner of the Five Spot) thought I was just trying to get more money out of him."

The Five Spot job got them into the Newport Festival (George Wein's gift to George Wein) and a Verve recording. Dennis' first date, however, was the later Transition record with the Cecil Taylor Quartet with Steve Lacey, soprano sax, and Buell Neidlinger, bass.

"I got a few jobs after that . . . a lot of rock and roll gigs . . . I even went back to calypso gigs. I've only recorded with Cecil and Gil Evans' big band. I've made four records with Cecil but not all of them are released. Maybe they all won't be. I worked with Jimmy Giuffre for a while at the Five Spot, and with Wilbur Ware at Birdland.

"But Blakey's my favorite. I like those other cats Philly (Joe Jones) and Max, (Roach); and Billy Higgins and Eddie Blackwell among the younger cats. But Blakey really moves me. A lot of people can play paradiddles and rudiments, but Art gets deep . . . I mean savage. Maybe because I'm from the West Indies and those people play like that, really pure and raw. They play what they hear. That's what I want.

"Elvin [Jones] too. He's really got himself together in the last years. Those little intricate figures and weird riffs. He plays right on Trane. He sounds like a brushfire back of Trane.

"Billy Higgins and Blackwell got a lot going. I used to go to Blackwell's house and listen and he'd show me things. But he used to get bugged at me cause I can't read. I don't really want to learn either! I want to play what I hear, you know, what I got in here.

"I dig Ornette's group . . . he knocks me out. I liked it better when he had Blackwell or Higgins, though. Ornette's and Cecil's music really open your ears. Sometimes I hear things I've never heard before. And they both get off into their instruments. They really go off into trances when they play, and that's beautiful to see.

"I used to get bugged because all I wanted to do was play that regular stuff. But the more I played the more I understood and the more I wanted to play. You gotta listen to those cats to understand them.

"I'd like to get strong and get control over the drums. I gotta get the physical thing taken care of. I don't have control over the instrument. I'm fighting, everytime I sit down. When I was playing steadily I had it going, but now I feel kinky. I need to practice by myself. You hear a whole lot of other things. It's like experimenting."

Right now, Dennis is down at The White Whale Coffee Shop on East Tenth Street, playing with two other rising heavyweights, Archie Shepp and Don Cherry. But the Whale is dark a lot and empty, except for the really righteous, most of the time. And when the junkies come round in hordes, to bolster the audience, everybody gets the shakes . . . heat lives off joints like this.

Talking to Dennis one has the feeling that he is somehow not really sure that he is the straight up tough guy he actually is on drums. He seems not to be certain, or maybe it's just the stackup of dreary tenements and beatout folks makes any "success story" seem very very shaky. And even when Dennis is working, he knows it's a very brief shot, and that soon he will be sitting back up on 118th Street without even anything to play on.

But when you see and hear him play, there is no doubt in your mind. This young man can really smoke. He has short powerful arms, somewhat reminiscent of Blakey, with the left stick held almost vertically. He makes a stabbing motion at the skin, rather than a regular "legitimate" stroke . . . it causes a surging, singing, eratic popping sound, an unusual accent to all his work. Dennis is heard to his best advantage on Cecil Taylor's *Looking Ahead*. Just try it for size.

"When I was young and fucking myself up (I got kicked out of high school for being 'too wild' . . . I was young and confused) these people around here used to tell me, 'Why don't you do something with yourself.' But when I started going down in the basement practicing every day . . . they started saying I was going crazy. My mother even went to the landlord and got me out. Everybody around here's on relief so they don't do anything all day. They hear it, when I practice. I had a place downtown practicing, but when I went to Germany I lost it . . . that's why I'm up here now . . . doing nothing."

*Note: Dennis Charles was one of the players named by me as avant-garde in 1961. Since leaving Cecil Taylor's group Dennis has had a variety of jobs, but has never made the breakthrough his talent should have made easy. But then, even the acknowledged innovators of the new music, or of the old music for that matter . . . wait a minute, let's say most black people . . . haven't made any money breakthroughs or fame breakthroughs either.*

# 1963

## New York Loft and Coffee Shop Jazz

*When this article was written the new music was being heard publicly almost not at all. Artists' lofts on the lower East Side and a few semi-legal operations in coffee shops were literally the only places one could hear the music.*

*Today, times have gotten generally better. Ornette, after coming out of retirement made a triumphant European tour, made a couple of critically acclaimed records, and now works, I would suppose, when he wants to. Shepp works from time to time; Cecil and Albert Ayler have started to appear at occasional large hall concerts, and both have had European tours of some significance. Sun-Ra, at this writing, was working Monday nights with his big band ("Astro-Infinity Music") at Slug's, in the East Village.*

*Slug's seems to be the only New York nite spot that hires the new musicians with any kind of consistency. Although Ornette (and of course, John Coltrane) have both been at the Village Vanguard.*

*But there has definitely been a general opening for the New Music, an opening that has permitted quite a few recordings to be made and has allowed some of the name musicians to work . . . though few regularly . . . but there is still not a lot of money or a lot of jobs being spread around.*

LJ Mar 66

IT WAS Martin Williams who recently called attention to the fact that one of the reasons the New York jazz scene was in such bad shape was because there were simply not enough clubs who wanted to feature the youngest and most exciting musicians. Of course, Coltrane and Rollins could play pretty much where they wanted, but when The Jazz Gallery closed down last year, and the Five Spot had to move, almost everyone associated with contemporary jazz felt the pinch.

But even when The Gallery was open, only rarely was there a chance of getting to hear any really exciting music. Of course Monk came through, and Coltrane and Rollins had been there, and if you were lucky you got to see them three or four times. But the majority of the attractions at The Gallery were those *names* that mean more to columnists and people in the entertainment world, than they do to the serious jazz public. The clubs downtown, like The Gallery and the Five Spot, and even the Half-Note and the Village Gate, under the best circumstances, by and large do not attract the kind of audiences that want to listen to Lambert, Hendricks and Bavan, or even Dave Brubeck. (In fact, I think that the Christmas when The Gallery brought Brubeck in they lost heaps of money, though the next week or so when Dave appeared at the uptown Basin Street club, he broke all records.) But I have been impressed for a long time now with the fact that the jazz club owner is the only entrepreneur who knows absolutely nothing about the product he is peddling. And I have suggested many times to my friends, that some Samaritan ought to put out a jazz club owners' consumer's report to better equip these naifs in the handling of their own businesses. I am not necessarily saying anything derogatory about L, H & B or Brubeck; it just seems to me a simple enough observation if one frequents any of these clubs with any regularity and knows the audience one is likely to find in them.

The Five Spot had been the place one expected to see the younger musicians perform. It seemed like it was going to be a latter day Royal Roost for young musicians like Ornette Coleman, Cecil Taylor, Eric Dolphy, Ted Curson, Oliver Nelson, Archie Shepp, Don Cherry, Billy Higgins, etc., as well as a place where one could hear older musicians like Monk, Coltrane and Rollins. But after a promising period, such was not the case. In a city that is just bursting at the seams with young cooking musicians, the Spot seemed content to lay with Roland Kirk. Monk, Coltrane and Rollins made their appearances at the Village Gate, a huge cavelike gymnasium where the other half of the bill was likely to be a *really* sick comedian or an African pop musician.

The Half Note seemed and seems intent on featuring Zoot Sims and Al Cohn most of the time, or "mixed groups" from out of town; and the Village Vanguard is a luxury affair where sometimes, between various entertainments, one can see Miles Davis or The M.J.Q. for the price of a tweed suit. It is an uptown club downtown. The clubs "uptown" or midtown that once were more closely associated with jazz are generally given over to popular entertainments . . . although at this writing The Jazz Corner of the World, Birdland,[1] has made some moves to change their Count Basie-Dinah Washington-Maynard Ferguson, etc. approach and have gotten Thelonius Monk and John Coltrane past Pee Wee Marquette to signal that club's possible reorientation.* The clubs way uptown, in Harlem, are usually into their "organ trio" bags.

But whatever specific penchant the owners of these various clubs may show, there seems, quite frankly, no way to get them interested in hiring men like Coleman, Taylor or any of the younger musicians associated with what's been called "the new thing." Most of these musicians get no work

* Now closed.

at all, except now and then a party or session in somebody's loft. But a few have begun to explore the possibility of playing in the coffee shops of Greenwich Village and the lower East Side. One of the first coffee houses to feature good jazz by younger musicians was The White Whale on East 10th Street. Trumpeters Don Cherry and Ted Curson led a few groups there, so did drummers Dennis Charles and Ed Blackwell, as well as saxophonist Archie Shepp and pianists Sonny Clark and Freddie Redd. The place was small and the coffee was terrible, but the music was usually very very good. And The Whale became, quite easily, one of the few places around New York where it was possible to hear good young musicians who were not playing merely to better their standards of living.

Other coffee houses around The Village and the lower East Side picked up on The Whale's policies very quickly, even though the Police and Fire Departments did every thing they could do to discourage the trend. (They finally discouraged The Whale right out of business. It seems that New York police and firemen become extraordinarily "efficient" when it becomes known that the money that is being spent at some coffee shop to see some young musician is money that could well be going to some larger local entertainment institution.) Take 3, a "coffee house theater," was one of the coffee shops that responded quickly, hiring Cecil Taylor's trio (Jimmy Lyons, alto and Sonny Murray, drums) for an extended stay. Since Taylor has returned from Europe he has gone back to this club, and it's still possible at this writing to go down there and hear him, i.e., some of the most awesomely exciting jazz being made in this country, and for a dollar. The only liability with this setup, of course, is that whatever this coffee shop is paying Taylor, it's certainly not enough. The money is elsewhere.

The Playhouse Coffee Shop was another place to bring in vital jazz. Though I didn't hear him, a great many people I respect told me that weird Sun-Ra (whom I had always thought of as a kind of "modernistic" faddist) had gotten a really swinging group together and was turning The Playhouse out every night of the week. The Cafes Avital and Metro, both on the East Side, each had the Archie Shepp-Bill Dixon Quartet working there for a while. Shepp is one of the freshest tenor voices I've heard, combining the furor of the Coltrane approach with the solid tone and ageless blues genius of a Ben Webster. And the only places one is usually able to hear him (aside from an ill-fated concert I sponsored up at The Maidman Theatre on 42nd Street last year, where Archie got a fine group together with trombonist Bernard McKinney along with a group led by Ted Curson which featured a very good young alto man named Pat Patrick) and other young musicians like him are the coffee shops or in somebody's loft. [Harout's, The Speakeasy, The Ninth Circle, The Cinderella Club, The Center, are some other small non-jazz clubs that still feature good jazz from time to time.]

Almost concomitantly with the development of jazz coffee houses (an idea, by the way, which is still not completely off the ground by any means or set up as well as it could be), another manifestation of New York's messed-up jazz scene was the beginning of loft jazz, i.e., not just sessions, but formally arranged concerts in lofts featuring some of the very best young New York based musicians. For the concerts, very little advertising is used due to the extremely limited finances at the sponsors' disposal (and the sponsors are in a great many instances the musicians themselves); one small ad is placed in the *Village Voice,* and a few hand-lettered signs are posted in important places all over the downtown area. But there are almost always very enthusiastic and empathetic, if not crushingly huge, audiences who respond. And they are usually treated to very exciting jazz. A kind of jazz that is getting increasingly more difficult to find in any regular jazz club in New York. As critic Williams said, what these club owners don't realize is that audiences change, and now, certainly in New York, there is a growing younger jazz audience who doesn't especially want to spend any money to hear the tired sounds the clubs are sponsoring.

Of the loft concerts, two of the most recent, and undoubtedly the best, I've heard have featured the same group: a "pick-up" trio composed of Don Cherry, Wilbur Ware and drummer, Billy Higgins. Hearing this group, one could only wish that they could somehow remain together. The music they made was simply beautiful. Each man is a very singular stylist and each is deeply intent on a great measure of extremely personal expression, but they played together as if they had to. It was extraordinary jazz. At the first concert featuring this group, which was held in a large loft on Great Jones Street, with people sitting in wooden folding chairs or squatting on the floor, the music was so lovely, there was almost no sound from the surprisingly large audience. But each solo was wildly applauded, and I'm sure the musicians could feel how direct an impact their music was making. Later in the evening a guitarist came up and played an Indian Raga, and Cherry and Higgins improvised against its fixed metres producing a music of startling freshness. A tall young alto player, John Tchicai, sat in with the original group for the last few numbers and brought the audience to its feet. Even though he is a Negro, Tchicai is a Danish citizen. He plays the alto like he wanted to sound like Coleman Hawkins playing like Ornette Coleman. But he sounds mostly like nothing you've heard before. There's no doubt in my mind that a lot more people are going to hear him very soon.

The other loft concert featured the Cherry-Ware-Higgins trio on the placards, but most of the times Henry Grimes played bass for Don and Billy. But they were still marvelous, and while Wilbur Ware's bass playing is something that makes me go home and try to write poems, Grimes was more than adequate. Another group on the bill was the Archie

Shepp-Bill Dixon Sextet, this time featuring the new man, Tchicai, on alto, and Charles Moffet, Ornette Coleman's last drummer. They ranted and raved, and had everyone in the audience stomping their feet and popping their fingers. There was a long solo of Shepp's that almost cracked my head open.

Still another feature of this last concert, and one of the most improbable treats I've had in some time, was the "return of Earl Coleman," as it was advertised on the few posters a couple of girls pinned up in bars and coffee shops. I have a .78 of Earl singing "Dark Shadows" with Charlie Parker, which I play every so often, but I don't know of anyone who's heard Coleman sing in person in years. But he was very much in person at this concert, which was held at a loft down on Clinton Street, which is deep on the lower East Side where nobody lives but poor and new Americans or artists. Wilbur Ware backed Earl up with the wildest accompaniment behind a singer I've ever heard, and Earl's voice seemed as good as it was in the old days.

Flasks (either formal or informal) seemed the most ubiquitous collation at the lofts, even though the Clinton Street people served free coffee and even some sandwiches. The admission this time was $1.50, which was money well spent. And many serious young jazz listeners now seem more willing to go sit on the floor in a loft and hear good music than go to the formal clubs downtown and hear well-known chumps, or travel uptown and get pushed by Pee Wee Marquette.

Williams was right, the jazz audience, at least here in New York, is changing, in fact, has changed a great deal already. One of the formal jazz clubs had better take this change into consideration when hiring their talent and get some of the exciting younger musicians into their clubs. There's a lot of them around The Apple now, who could even be used as the second group opposite some *name*. It's bad enough to let so much talent go to waste, but it's worse to let it starve.

# 1962

## Introducing Bobby Bradford

BOBBY BRADFORD represents part of a "new wave" of young and extremely talented trumpet players who've sprung up recently. Along with Don Cherry, Freddie Hubbard, Richard Williams, Lee Morgan, Ted Curson, Don Ellis, Marcus Belgrave and a few others, Bobby Bradford seems bent on forging an entirely individual approach to jazz trumpet playing. Each of these players in his own way seems to be a trumpet player who will be an influence of the future. And while a few of them are still pretty dependent on some parent style (Williams, for instance, still seems to be prying himself loose from the Clifford Brown style, and his efforts are admirable), for the most part these young men are beginning to play their own music. Bobby Bradford seems to be one of the most individual of these young musicians.

Bobby was born in Cleveland, Mississippi, twenty-seven years ago—he adds, "about a hundred miles from the all-Negro town of Mound Bayou." The family moved to Los Angeles when he had reached the fifth grade, but remained only one year and then moved on to Detroit for another year. The Bradfords and Bobby finally moved to Dallas in 1946 where, except for Bobby, they still live today.

"My people tried to get me to play piano when I was a kid. I had to give it up, though. The cats were telling me all that stuff about only sissies played piano, and what not.

"I started playing trumpet in 1949. You won't believe how
it happened. There was this fellow across the street who had
a trumpet and played it all the time. After a while, I used to
go over and bug him about it. I mean I was constantly going
over to his house. You know, like, show me how to do this
and let me blow it . . . and all that. Finally, Christmas of
1948 I got a watch and before you know it that guy had my
watch and I had his trumpet."

By September of 1949 Bobby was playing with the school
band at Lincoln High School. (Cedar Walton, the pianist,
and James Clay, the much-talked-about tenor man, were also
at Lincoln at the time.) Bobby is what could be called a self-
taught musician. "In Dallas," Bobby remembers, "there was
a guy whose father owned a music store who used to teach
me a little about the horn. You know, little tips about playing. At the time, I was working in my father's drugstore and
used to keep the horn under the counter. I practiced between customers.

"In high school they wouldn't even let me take band. My
home room teacher made me take all the academic courses,
like Latin and geometry, because she thought I was bright.
But, on the horn, I'm mostly self-taught. I learned scales
first, then I just figured out the chromatics. I played scales
when I was practicing because I knew when you were learning an instrument you were supposed to play scales."

After high school, Bobby went to Tillotson College in
Austin for a year and a half, then he joined the Air Force.
Even though he stayed in the service almost four years, forty-
six months to be exact, Bobby never managed to leave Texas.
He did, however, play with a number of good Air Force
bands and picked up a great deal of valuable musical experience. When he finally got out of the Air Force, Bobby left
Texas and went to Los Angeles. He was working in a de-
partment store and jamming around town at the various ses-

sions when he ran into Ornette Coleman, a musician he had
played with in Texas a few years before. Bobby joined
Ornette's newly formed quintet and they managed to get a
few jobs in the red-light district of Los Angeles. However,
when Ornette finally made the move East, Bobby didn't
make it because he wanted to be sure he could support his
growing family. (That family now includes a wife and three
children.) But this summer Bobby finally did come to New
York to join Ornette's new group, after Don Cherry left to
form his own trio.

Bobby's style is unabashedly romantic, i.e., he does not
always go to the blues bag for the materials of his improvisations. But his use of "non-jazz" elements in his solos is usually fresh and always interesting. For instance, many times
listening to Bobby play I am struck by his ability to sound as
if he were playing "popular" music. The improvisation is
always very melodic and lyrical (as if there were actual
words that could go along with the solo). His tone is
rounder and more lush than most of the Miles Davis-influ-
enced younger trumpet players. However, the tone is not as
big and brash as the Dizzy and Clifford fanciers, e.g., Freddie Hubbard or Richard Williams. It is a torchy lyric sound,
broad, but almost tender. And it moves in beautiful contrast
to Ornette Coleman's jagged, cutting speeches.

Asked about influences, Bobby was quick to answer, "I
respect all the greats. I thought Fats (Navarro) was God.
Dizzy was a bitch . . . but I liked Fats. He had a big beautiful sound. I liked Miles, too. I was a Miles fanatic for a while
. . . copied all his solos. Dizzy, Miles, Art Farmer, I like all
those cats . . . but I never really wanted to play like any of
them. I mean when my playing was being molded, I wanted
to play like Fats. But I don't think you can play like anybody
but yourself. People say Sonny Stitt sounds like Bird . . . but
I don't think so.

"Living in the South all your life you never get to hear the greats. Except on records. Just occasionally on some tour, maybe Bird and Diz in a package with Stan Kenton. That's why it was such a gas to come here and see all these guys I'd idolized, in person . . . like John Lewis or Kenny Dorham or Roy Haynes. You know I had a picture in my mind of all these musicians. You know . . . what they looked like. Charlie Rouse looked sort of like I thought he'd look. Miles didn't look, up close, anything like I thought he'd look.

"And people really sound so different in person, too. The funny thing is that people trying to play like Miles, for instance, by listening to records, without ever really hearing Miles, are all messed up. You could really get frustrated. I mean, even Miles can't play the way he does on records. You know there's a lot of electricity and engineers working away, too."

Bobby's ideas about music, and especially his own music and Ornette Coleman's music are very vital and well thought out. "I always thought of the trumpet as a melodic horn. And I think there's a way to play very melodically even way up tempo, but I don't think I've quite gotten into it yet.

"Now that I've got a chance to play, I want to play what I hear. It's a great feeling to get on the stand and play what *you* hear—not just licks, or other cats' licks.

"People are always asking me, even musicians, questions about Ornette's music. They come up to me and ask things like—Can Ornette play tunes like "Tea For Two"?—a dumb tune like that. I guess it's because Ornette's got such a free sense of rhythm and harmony. And he's not in the minor 7th bag all the time. A lot of people can only resolve their tunes one certain way . . . these little two- and four-bar phrases. Sometimes Ornette gets some beautiful three-bar things going. He's even got an eleven-and-a-half-bar blues. A beautiful thing. His tunes are not written with chords in mind. The tunes are like a stimulus to get the music to go in a certain melodic and rhythmic direction. They're not written to get you to go back. People think he's just playing random notes. But there is a logical harmonic sequence to what Ornette plays. He doesn't play any favorites with notes, though. I guess maybe it might seem ridiculous to people who haven't played this way. But it's pretty stupid to put people down without even knowing what they're doing. I'll tell you, if a guy came along playing a coke bottle, I'd wait until I heard him before I laughed."

Bobby has yet to record with the new Ornette Coleman quartet. (The group now includes C. M. Moffett on drums and Jimmy Garrison, bass.) But there are plans in the works now for a date sometime this fall. In the meantime, Bobby is working with Coleman at New York's famous Five Spot Cafe, six nights a week, and there is also the possibility of a European tour, to which Bobby is looking forward a great deal. He is also hoping to get his family to New York as soon as possible . . . now that he's working regularly. "You know," Bobby asked, genuinely mystified, "I wonder how all these musicians can keep up their techniques in New York, because most of them aren't working. It's really amazing. I don't have to tell you how good it is to be working. And it's really a challenge to play with Ornette, but I like it."

*Bobby Bradford never did record with the Ornette Coleman group. Not very long after this interview, he returned to Texas with his family—where he is now.*

# 1962

## Present Perfect (Cecil Taylor)

*THE GIL EVANS ORCHESTRA Into The Hot;* Impulse
A-9; (On John Carisi's compositions) John Glasel, Joe
Wilder ("Moon Taj" only), Doc Severinsen ("Angkor
Wat" only), Clark Terry ("Barry's Tune" only), trumpets;
Urbie Green, Bob Brookmeyer ("Moon Taj" and "Barry's
Tune" only), trombones; Harvey Phillips, tuba; Jim Buf-
fington ("Angkor Wat" only), French horn; Gene Quill,
Phil Woods, alto saxophones; Barry Galbraith, guitar; Eddie
Costa, piano and vibes; Milt Davis ("Angkor Wat" only),
Art Davis ("Moon Taj" and "Barry's Tune" only), bass;
Osie Johnson, drums. (On Cecil Taylor's compositions)
("Pots" and "Bulbs") Taylor, piano; Jimmy Lyons, alto
saxophone; Archie Shepp, tenor saxophone; Henry Grimes,
bass; Jimmy Murray, drums; ("Mixed") add Ted Curson,
trumpet; Roswell Rudd, trombone.
 "Moon Taj," "Angkor Wat," "Barry's Tune" (John
Carisi)
 "Pots," "Bulbs," "Mixed" (Cecil Taylor)

THIS RECORD, for the Cecil Taylor compositions included, is one of the three most important records to be
released this year (the other two being Ornette Coleman's
*Free Jazz* and John Coltrane's *Live*). And not so strangely,
each of these records shows a totally different yet completely valid stance and direction for contemporary jazz. In
one sense, however, Coleman and Taylor are closer to each

other in the implications of their moves than they are to
Coltrane. Taylor and Coleman represent beginnings, new
shapes to Afro-American musical tradition, while Coltrane
represents a maturation, or *ending*, to a particular kind of
jazz. Coltrane seeks with each new onslaught to completely
destroy the popular song. Taylor and Coleman are proceeding as if Coltrane's work had been completed long ago. *Live*,
a rudimentary blues, is mysterious to ears listening for the
thumping pretty changes of "My Favorite Things." As for
*Free Jazz* and Cecil's music on this album, it will take years
before most "change-ears" even admit Cecil and Ornette are
playing jazz. (But then there are still critics who talk about
the "heresy of bebop.")

*Free Jazz* is so important because it reestablishes the absolute hegemony of improvisation in jazz. *Live*, because it
proves that blues can still function on any level as an
*autonomous* music (and is not limited merely to playing
funky versions of "Melancholy Baby)". Taylor's contribu-
tions on this album redemonstrate that the gifted jazz
soloist, even the innovator, can function on a highly creative
level in the context of formal composition. And that the
really swinging ensemble style of jazz playing is still useful.
So that it would seem that in a sense Ornette takes on the
role of a latterday Armstrong, and Taylor the mantle of one,
J. R. Morton. Ornette, even though he is a gifted composer,
is an innovator because of his *playing*, his approach to the
jazz solo, and by implication to the whole of the music. Cecil
is a fantastic soloist, but his compositions demonstrate how
this changed music will be preserved as a notated music.
Cecil seems much more conscious of the possibility of his
music being played *by others* than Coleman. Ornette's
compositions, like Charlie Parker's, are issued from a musical mind much more controlled by the exigencies of solo
performance, and the constant variation of purely extempor-
ized music. Most of his tunes seem to have come together *after*

he has improvised them. Taylor's seem much more works of composition, rather than notated solos. Already people like Gil Evans (who had little to do with the music on this album—one of the musicians told me that the most he did was go out and bring back sandwiches) want to record Cecil's compositions . . . can visualize them as pieces for larger groups. Ornette's tunes, because they are so purely the result of a soloist rather than a composer, probably seem more remote. One thing Coltrane has in common with these other two men is his ability to re-create a jazz anarchic as the blues shout. A jazz where the "changes" are formal only insofar as they are determined by the defining *rhythm* and whatever emotional predictability the total character of the music implies. As blues, "a music with or without occasion," certainly undetermined in any serious area by the limitations of the thirty-two bar popular music form. But Coltrane, of course, is still bothered by, hems himself in because of, the active residue of that music as it manifests itself in his interminable obsession with the structure of regular recurring chord lines. One gets the feeling that Coltrane would like to take every chord he has ever heard and rephrase and restructure it, hearing the chord in every other form possible. The frighteningly limiting scale of "My Favorite Things" is Ancient Musik to Coleman and Taylor. It was a useful scale to Trane because the changes are so regular they implied a rhythm he must be enamored of. He has done "Greensleeves" and "Inchworm" in that same image. Coltrane's salvation will only come as murderer, or anarchist, whose anarchy seems so radical because references to the "old music" still remain. *Live* is a case in point.

It seems that Taylor and Coleman are dropped on us right out of bebop. Their indebtedness as soloists to Monk and Powell on the one hand and Charlie Parker on the other are constantly acknowledged. It would seem that they never accepted the post-bop brain rot of *cool* or the misguided ancestor worship of funk-groove-soul, but took the new learning of bop and put it to logical uses. People will use Coltrane to beat Ornette and Cecil over the head, not understanding that actually Trane functions as their hired assassin. He is using the various post-bop reactions to prepare, as it were, an area for Taylor and Coleman. And it is his power as a soloist that makes his efforts so meaningful. Taylor and Coleman do not have to worry about the meaningless antics of a Cannonball Adderley when there is Coltrane's continuous public confession spelling out how close to oblivion musicians like Cannonball (or Art Blakey or Bobby Timmons or The Jazztet) had brought jazz. (But the chief assassin might yet prove to be Sonny Rollins, who had developed a "perfect" music, and has now—at least in performance—abandoned it in favor of a beautiful efficient "nihilism." His group is also one that might be capable of finally forcing understanding of *contemporary* jazz on the melancholy baby crowd. Don Cherry and Billy Higgins, graduates of the first and meanest of the Coleman groups, are proving very strong influences on the shape Sonny's new music is taking. Now that *The Bridge* is out of the way and Victor and some new buyers are convinced that Sonny can play pretty, the recorded music will soon come closer to the performed. There will be screams of agony and cries of "Traitor!" when the live session from the Village Gate is released. I wait impatiently, and only hope that I am asked to identify some of the bodies.)

Cecil's tunes on this album create, by their sincere attempts at perfection of a form that is still not completely understood, a musical environment that will make the fingerpoppers shudder. It is an orchestral language that Cecil is pointing towards; a language that still conceives of verb force, i.e., the solo exclamation made fierce by improvisation. It will be as complete a language as Ellington's, with the loose swinging ensemble style that made Basie's band the real haven for the soloist. On "Bulbs," the ensemble sets the orchestral tone of the music and establishes the harmonic depth. Then Cecil, after serving as the deepest harmonic color, leaps into the front and using the rhythm section as a flag, makes a solo that seems as if the "orchestra" had proposed it. (Although this group on "Bulbs" and "Pots" is only a quintet, it sounds consistently like a very large group.) Altoist Lyons seems sure that Bird still fits this music, and he is right more often than not. But it is tenor saxophonist Shepp who is the most impressive horn on this tune. Who ever thought that Ben Webster and John Coltrane could show up sounding so completely like someone else. Shepp has taken older influences and made them fit the emotional scope of this music, and he is certainly not afraid to play "low down." Bass player Grimes holds the group together, and collects Cecil's diverse rhythmic pronouncements perfectly.

"Mixed" seems to me the most ambitious and adventurous composition on the album. Two other horns are added, to swell the group to seven—trumpeter Ted Curson, who sets the mood and emotional term of the initial section of the pierce, along with Taylor's lush and sweeping piano and the constant restatement of this theme by Shepp, beneath the piano. The other horn is the trombone of Roswell Rudd, which adds a body to the music that really gives it an orchestral sound. The piece itself seems formally divided into repeated sections. The first, a kind of tortured ballad, on which Shepp, Taylor and Curson are featured as separate but contrastingly related solo voices. The second section, which also serves as the release, or launching pad from which the actual solos are sprung, is a tight thrashing blues riff. The kind of riff, at least in the manner of its use, that reminds one so much of the earlier Basie bands, where the riff was the triggering form that demanded the relief and resolution of the solos. Taylor's solos after these riffs, and as they occur throughout the composition, almost shaping the rhythm, are superb.

"Pots" contains some of the best Taylor piano on the entire album. The initial solo is the kind of scrambling yet precise pianistics that are Taylor's patented device, and is strictly virtuoso, but Taylor, Coltrane, Rollins and Coleman are among the few musicians who can make technical exercises emotional experiences. Drummer Murray also has his best hearing on this effort, as well as alto saxophonist Jimmy Lyons.

Taylor and the others are making music that is exactly where we are. It is as exact in its emotional registrations and as severely contemporary in its aesthetic as any other Western art. It is a shame that there are so many hobbyists, social workers, and men-whose-best-friends-are-X's connected in one way or another with the music, because it does obfuscate the area in which the work of the legitimate innovators is being done. But what can you say of a society that sends Benny Goodman and Robert Frost to Russia as cultural avants. I am convincing myself that it is the least of our worries. (Addendum: John Carisi's music is *cool progressive*, you dig?)

# 1962

## Cecil Taylor

*The World of Cecil Taylor* (Candid 8006); Taylor, piano; Archie Shepp, tenor (on "Air" and "Lazy Afternoon" only); Buell Neidlinger, bass; Dennis Charles, drums.

"Air," "This Nearly Was Mine," "Port of Call," "E.B.," "Lazy Afternoon"

THE FIRST THING this album made me think of, especially the title, was an idea I've been trying to work out for quite a while now. Is there really a "world" of Cecil Taylor, or to put it exactly the way I'd been thinking about it: Has Cecil Taylor really succeeded in finding a separate or *new* kind of jazz music, or is he merely applying an amazingly fresh musical personality to a quite "traditional" form? Actually, on the basis of this album, I would have to say the latter idea seems true.

For instance, the best tune on the album, "This Nearly Was Mine," is a tune that under ordinary circumstances is one of the most terrifyingly maudlin pop tunes of our time. But Taylor seems to come to the tune with this in mind because he almost completely rearranges the melodic, harmonic and rhythmic devices of the tune and succeeds in making a music that is so personal and intimate as to give one the feeling that the original "This" never really existed, except as a kind of dyspeptic nightmare. But the real point of this is that Taylor can and does go to old forms and old nightmares and make his own music. A music which I am beginning to think is about as "traditional" as any really fresh and exciting jazz music can be. And by traditional here I mean not reaction or academicism, but the *use* of materials and ideas that are perhaps cultural inheritances . . . things Taylor has taken from the inordinately vital "history" of jazz and worked over into something for himself.

As another for instance, this same tune, "This," as I said a frighteningly fragile piece of "midtown" fluff, Cecil has made into a subtle but genuinely bluesy blues. The kind of delicate blues that Montana Taylor could do so well. The "blue" insistence . . . one of accretion rather than immediate overstatement (the kind of overstatement I have come to call superfunk).

But the other tunes on this album are admirable, too. "Port of Call" and "Lazy Afternoon" next in excellence (to "This"). Taylor's rhythmic sense is perhaps the thing that I become most excited by. He seems to get the rhythm right up in the melodic surface of his music. And this is seen immediately in tunes of his own like "Port of Call" or "E.B." (On an earlier album of Taylor's, *Looking Ahead*, which I think contains perhaps his best recorded efforts, one of the originals "Of What" shows exactly how melody and rhythm can be integrated to form a musical object of extraordinary power.) But this insistence, i.e., the insertion of the rhythmic pulse of the music directly into the melody is not really innovation. (Although most of the fashionable funk merchants have almost forgotten that the rhythmic elements of a music must *move*, even flow . . . not in texture, but as far as the *ideas* these elements contain. I mean a static rhythm that is related to its melodic surface only by arbitrary arrangement produces nothing of musical value, albeit it might increase someone's standard of living.) Thelonius Monk and Charlie Parker both utilized this concept in their writing and playing, as did most of the boppers. Ornette Coleman, Taylor, Eric Dolphy and some others are trying to reempha- size this attack today. (And it is a very simple conclusion that so-called scat singing, which the boppers took up and modernized, attempted to make melody out of rhythmic elements of the music.)

The rest of Taylor's group show themselves as fine musi- cians as well. I think that the drummer, Dennis Charles, is one of the most interesting young drummers around, and he certainly will get even better. The tenor saxophonist, Archie Shepp, is putting some Coltrane influences to good use, even though I am not quite convinced he has come to understand Taylor's music rhythmically, as yet. But he has at least shown that he is capable of moving in pretty fancy musical circles. Bass player Buell Neidlinger gets a bigger and more musical sound each time I hear him, though there is nothing on this album from him that matches his fantastic perform- ance on the record I spoke of earlier, *Looking Ahead*, except perhaps some parts of "This."

One final note. There's a little group of regulars walking around nowadays saying they can't "pop their fingers" to Taylor's music (or Ornette Coleman's, etc.). To them I can only say, there's definitely something wrong with your fin- gers.

*Photo: Daniel Dawson*

ORNETTE COLEMAN

*Photo: Daniel Dawson*

ALAN SILVA, DWANE ALSTON,
SONNY MURRAY, JIMMY OWENS, RUSSELL LYLE

*Photo: Daniel Dawson*

**PHAROAH SANDERS**

Photo: *Daniel Dawson*

SUN-RA

# 1964

## Apple Cores #1

*Introduction to Applecores/*
  The following pieces were written as casual columns, for *Down Beat*, *Wild Dog*. They appear here somewhat edited, but essentially the same.
  They are meant not only as passing identifications and registrations but as handholds into the new music and re-actions to Jazz-America in general.

LJ Mar 66

WHERE, FINALLY, will the new musicians find to play? The club owners who are, at best, "hip" bartenders, are not really "responsible." They don't know anything (except the sound of falling coin, and recently, unable to discover "where the jazz public went to," they haven't even been able to get into that . . . e.g., weekend-only policies, rock 'n' roll, ragtime comedians, literate porgy and bess poetry readings . . . all have added little to the kitty, so wearily, they go back to their ol' jazz buddies). It's too bad, because now's the time, really, for some of these owners to start booking the newer groups, and pick up an audience that's just waiting for someplace to go. Coffee shops and lofts, as I mentioned in an earlier piece, have taken up some of the slack, but there are still too many originals walking around with just about no place to play.
  In line with first proposition, some citizens have tried to

organize jazz clubs, European style, to meet in lofts on weekends, with some kind of club structure, to make the whole thing "legal." Until there are public places, the music will have to be heard underground. Another idea was to start a church. I think seventeen citizens is all you need to start a religion or at least get a church cover story. The sanctified (holiness, pentecostal, God Christ, etc.) churches blow half the night. If you got a church sign, you can go into almost anything and the law will not be able to stop you.

One citizen recently gave a party at the old closed up Jazz Gallery. (Since JG days it has been umpteen unsuccessful coffee shops . . . the last being the Ski Lodge, so the place was outfitted in ski trappings, etc.) Albert Ayler with Sonny Murray and Gary Peacock was one group. Don Cherry sat in with them a great deal of the time, although he was leading another group. A lot of young musicians got a chance to play. Archie Shepp had a group that featured Allen Shorter on trumpet (Wayne's brother . . . and definitely, already, into as much as Wayne), Don Moore, who played bass with the New York Contemporary Five in Europe, and Edgar Bateman on drums. Cherry's group featured a very strong beautiful tenor player from Little Rock, Pharoah Sanders. I'd heard him a few months earlier in an East Side coffee shop with the Charles Moffat quartet, which featured Carla Bley on piano. Pharoah is out of the Coltrane bag, but that bag became bigger than Trane knew, a long time ago. Sanders is putting it together very quickly; when he does somebody will tell you about it. But he can play, right now. Paul Allen was the other horn in the group, and he can blow towards a smoother groove, but complicating . . . and probably still moving. Billy Higgins was the drummer and Jimmy Garrison also sat in half the night. There was a lot of very strong playing, a lot of beautiful images. It was even a good night.

On Monday and Friday afternoons, a practice big band under the "leadership" of Cedar Walton meets at the Five Spot. The musicians like Clifford Jordan, Roland Alexander, Pat Patrick, Don Moore, Frank Haines, Reggie Workman, Martin Banks, Clarence (C) Sharpe, Garnett Brown, Julian Priester, Tommy Turrentine, Pharoah Sanders, J. C. Moses and quite a few others have been coming by so far. One chart the band's playing is something by Clifford Jordan, like complicated Basie. Some other near-Basie charts are being gone over, too. But the whole idea's good, especially when so many players don't have a place to play otherwise.

CONSUMER'S GUIDE: A few very fine LP's to pass through my fingers recently (whether they are recent or not, but most are). *Evolution* (Blue Note 4153) which is a sextet led by Grachun Moncur, the critic's choice new star trombone. This is the core of the group (Jackie McLean, alto; Bobby Hutcherson, critics' new star vibes; Tony Williams, critics' new star drums) that played on Jackie Mc's last album *One Step Beyond* (Blue Note 4137), which is also a very very marvelous thing. On *Evolution*, Bob Crenshaw is the bassist, replacing Eddie Khan. Lee Morgan is added on trumpet, and he adds a lot, too. Some of the best Lee I've ever heard; all those quick, doodling phrases and tricky lipping, he makes into useful musical artifice on this, and singing! But the whole group is strong, and they give a fresh meaning to what them cats call "swinging." Jackie plays hard and raw the way he does, muscular and right up on the beat. He's been strong for a long time now. Tony Williams is already a master at what he does. Solos of his such as the one on "Saturday and Sunday", on the McLean side, or his work on "Air Raid" or "Evolution", on Moncur's date, show that he is well into his own thing. Williams breaks up rhythm into personal intervals, as pulse rather than beat, though the beat is finally there. Unlike another young drummer, Sonny Murray, who played with Cecil Taylor for four or five years, now with Albert Ayler, Gary Peacock and Don Cherry in Europe. Murray takes the drums to, as far as I've heard, an even farther shore. Murray's intervals, his pulsations, are completely "arbitrary." Williams' only seem to be . . . but, to be sure, they are very different drummers, and each is saying something very important. In fact they are probably the two most exciting younger drummers on the scene right now. (Some others I'd name, of course Billy Higgins, Dennis Charles, Eddie Blackwell, Joe Chambers, J. C. Moses, Charles Moffat.) Where Williams "places" his sounds, i.e., arranges them in relation to the whole musical organism, his solos still seem at times almost completely autonomous (e.g., "Saturday and Sunday"), but there is always a carrying rhythmic drive that makes the solo an ever-changing commentary on the rest of the music, as well as serving to "balance" the improvisation. Murray, however, does not place his sounds, he creates the drums as a complete musical entity, inseparable from the entire musical feeling, balanced only by the orderliness of the musician's deepest musical sensibility. Murray plays the drums without thought to serving any function except the complete freedom and spontaneity of his constant improvising. That is, Murray improvises "freely" throughout the tune and plays all the time, without any recourse to, say, the formal idea of rhythmic accompaniment. He doesn't "keep time," he makes, moves it.

One very fine example of Murray's playing can be heard on Albert Ayler's new album *Spirits* (Debut 146) which also features another Cleveland musician, Norman Howard, on trumpet and Henry Grimes and Earle Henderson alternating, as well as playing duets, on bass. (This is Ayler's second album on Debut, though distribution has been poor, the other being *My Name Is Albert Ayler* (Debut 140), which was recorded in Copenhagen in 1963, with Ayler on soprano

as well as tenor and Niels Bronsted, piano; Niels-Henning
Orsted Pedersen, bass; Ronnie Gardiner, drums.)

Anyone interested in hearing what's happening right now
in jazz ought to get these two albums. Ayler's playing, as I've
said before, is a revelation. Ayler's approach to music is similar to Murray's in the sense that both men are trying to play
themselves. The other musicians on *Spirits* also seem interested in getting to where they, themselves, are, rather than
just showing up "hip," playing all the accepted licks of the
day.

Trumpet player Norman Howard will make a lot of people
sit up and listen. His runs are piercing staccato blasts that
leave little room for charming ready-made quotes or fake
displays of easy virtuosity. Henry Grimes (dig especially
*Spirits*) can sound like a string quartet, but the complexity
and subtlety of his playing never obscures the hot rhythmic
core of his driving "accompaniments." One of the tunes,
"Witches and Devils," should frighten anyone given to mystical involvement or even simple impressionistic reaction. It is
a scary tune, going deep beneath what we say is real to that
other portion of our selves that is, finally, realer and much
less familiar.

On the album *My Name Is Albert Ayler*, Ayler plays with
a surprisingly good rhythm section made up of two Danes
and an American (Gardiner) who's been playing around
the Scandanavian countries for a few years. Albert's work
on soprano is almost as valuable as his work on tenor (dig
"Summertime" and "Green Dolphin Street"). The bassist,
Orsted Pedersen, shows up very well on this album . . .
his playing on "C.T." is very fine (Ayler's fantastic). But the
entire group had some strong empathy for Ayler, whose mad
runs, and huge exploding sound, sound even wilder with a
listening rhythm section: witness *Spirits*.

The word around now is listen to Betty Carter! She's gone
way past those Ray Charles duets. I heard a recent tape at

one citizen's house that was really something else, maybe
more than that. She also turned out a benefit this summer at
the Five Spot, singing with her own trio. Miss Carter seems
to hear her voice now more personally, as a human extension
of human feeling, rather than as say, some formal (revived)
artifact that must wade wearily through word after word of
essentially vapid "popular" songs. To say that she "uses her
voice like an instrument," is to cheapen her intent. She uses
her voice toward the limits of its physical (and emotional)
expressiveness . .. past mere melody, as a constantly stated,
recurring theme, to a way of collecting very hidden facets of
emotion by giving very individual (even as say our throats
are different sizes, and different sounds can be made to come
out of them) values to her notes, rests, slurs, etc. I mean, she
sounds very good.

Another very important young tenor player is Archie
Shepp who has just recently released half an LP, *Archie
Shepp and the Contemporary Five* (Savoy MG-12184). The
other half of the LP is taken up with a group led by trumpeter
Bill Dixon. The Shepp side, which features John Tchicai,
the Danish Negro alto saxophonist; Ronnie Boykins, bass;
Sonny Murray, drums; Ted Curson guest artist on two tunes
and Don Cherry the NYC5's regular trumpet player arriving
at the session for only one tune, "Consequences" (which
turned out to be the winner of the album), really contains
the serious business. Two of the tunes, "Where Poppies
Bloom" and "Like a Blessed Baby Lamb" are Shepp compositions, the other tune, "Consequences," was Cherry's. Archie
sounds lovely throughout the entire date, but on "Lamb" and
"Consequences" he really stretches out. He combines a big
wide elegant bluesiness with a rhythmic force that often has
people trying to connect him with Ben Webster . . . which is
no bad connection. But Archie has something to say which is
new and powerfully moving. John Tchicai makes music of a
very different nature than Shepp's, but it is also a very moving

music. Tchicai's playing, his approach to his horn, really fas-
cinates me. His tone is dry, acrid, incisive; his line spare and
lean, like himself; and his phrasing at times reminds one of
Mondrian's geometrical decisions, or lyrical syllogisms.
Where Shepp's intentions are usually immediately apparent,
sweet or nasty blues, though of a very wild contemporary
persuasion, Tchicai's ear leads him into subtleties of expression
where the "pure" blues feeling is replaced by a constantly
complicating musical/emotional tension which is "soulful"
because the player has a great deal of soul.

Shepp recently cut a side for Impulse,* which is supposed
to be released this winter. The date was made under John
Coltrane's "sponsorship" and features quite a few of Trane's
tunes. But Shepp has a great many lovely tunes of his own
and should be allowed to play them.

Biggest hole in the music scene continues to be caused by
the absence from it, publicly, of Ornette Coleman. (He has,
of course, been playing at home, and many of the young
musicians around New York come by his place to play. For
this reason, Ornette has one of the wildest tape collections of
new music around. He has also been learning to play the
trumpet and the violin, and is already past the purely technical and going straight on out.) Ornette, burned equally by
record companies, nightclub owners and jive promoters, is
trying to open his own place now . . . a place where not only
his music can be heard but also a lot of the other gifted but
publicly silent younger musicians. But, so far, he has had
little success. It's about time, I think, for the cooperative
jazz club, etc. to open. Musicians ought to get together and
"do it yourself." It would be a revolution on the jazz scene,
not to mention the whole entertainment economy. Musicians
playing for themselves . . . and playing exactly what they
want to. That would be the millennium, for real. But there are

* (*Four for Trane*)

very few people strong enough to see such a program
through.

More Consumer's Guide, in the big beat bag; Mary Wells
. . . "Oh, Little Boy" and "My Guy"; The Supremes . . .
"Where Did Our Love Go?" (which is really beautiful);
lovely Dionne Warwick . . . "Any Old Time of Day," and
please listen to "Walk On By." It will really turn you inside.
Also another of Dionne's "You'll Never Get to Heaven If You
Break My Heart." Wild group is Martha and the Vandellas
on "Heat Wave" and "A Love Like Yours."

There's a chance that National Educational Television
will put on a whole series of jazz programs, which might not
have to feature Al Hirt or Shorty Rogers. But seeing, like
they say, is believing.

# 1965

## Apple Cores #2

ESP RECORDS, new project gotten together by Bernard Stollman, promises to be one of the most valuable developments in contemporary jazz in some time. Stollman has so far made tapes and test discs of some of the most interesting new groups around this town, e.g., The New York Art Quartet, which is John Tchicai, alto; Roswell Rudd, trombone; Louis Worrell, bass (recently, Eddie Gomez); and drummer, Milford Graves, who must be heard at once. Graves might remind some well traveled citizen of Albert Ayler's drummer, Sonny Murray, because he keeps all his sound devices working almost continuously and simultaneously. But Graves has a rhythmic drive, a constant piling up of motor energies that makes him a distinct stylist. He is also beginning to use the Indian derived Tabla drum, as well as making innovations in cymbal playing, sometimes stroking the underside of the ride or crashing in such a way as to produce high-pitched whining, whistling sounds which punctuate percussion phrases like some Eastern string instrument. Graves studied for a long time with an Indian Tabla drummer, and for this reason the sound he gets from a snare drum seems completely different from the usual drum and bugle corps ratatat most drummers get.

Graves also plays a big part on another ESP side, made by young alto saxophonist Giuseppe Logan. (Logan also plays tenor and trumpet.) Logan has a quartet on this first side, Don Pullen, a pianist who might still be finding his own way by using a few Cecil Taylor forms to point out a personal direction, Eddie Gomez, bass and Milford Graves, drums and Tabla drums. On this record Logan seems to have been inspired by Indian music, although the backbone of this music is as Western as it has to be to remain jazzical. The names of the tunes on this side might give you an idea what these young men are into: "Tabla Suite," "Dance of Satan," "Dialogue," "Taneous," "Bleecker St. Partita." I've yet to hear Logan in person, but behind this record, I'll have to make it my business. This group along with another percussionist named Sahumba, will have a concert at Judson Hall, February 8.

Still another ESP "find" is altoist Byron Paul Allen, whose first side is called "Time Is Past." Allen's group is a trio with Theodore Robinson, percussion and Maceo Gilchrist, bass. This group already sounds like they've been together for a long time, that is, they already have a distinct and original sound form as a group. And Paul Allen is moving to become a deep thinker on his instrument, and we might not have long to wait. For instance, a statement he made, possibly to be included in any liner notes for this first album: "For musicians only: Time is not speed, it's distance, and sound is measured motion." Drummer Theodore Robinson also made a statement, which I think might tell you almost exactly where he is, or at least was, when he made it: "Since God has bestowed me with the want to execute the sound that I feel, I shall proceed." Go ahead.

ESP has also recorded tenor man Albert Ayler (who is just back from Europe and Cleveland, getting ready now to mess up a few people's minds. Now if Mr. Stollman is for real, we will soon have some heavy sounds to help us get through our stay in America.

Some words from tenor man Pharoah Sanders, whose own

first record (also recorded by ESP) will make believers out of a lot of people. "Accept everything. Accept other people just the way you accept yourself. If you're not playing you, you're playing somebody else's solo. You can be a taker or a giver. You can either be spiritual or something else. Music is a key to discipline in people. It can heal sick people. Music is like a spiritual thing. It's like an underworld thing. All creation is done by spiritual persons." Sanders music reinforces these statements.

Recently Sanders has been playing with drummer Rashid-Ali (who also plays trumpet) and trumpet player Dewey Johnson (who is also a very fine drummer). A concert, as part of a poetry reading sponsored by IN/FORMATION newspaper at the St. Marks Playhouse, brought together these three important young musicians plus a new alto player, Marion Brown, who is one of the most exciting horn players in New York today.

Brown is tenor man (Archie Shepp's "sideman") in the new group Shepp is putting together. Brown's style, while still formative, can be described as post-Coleman, but he is just beginning to stretch out, though he is, by most standards, already into something startlingly his own. Brown and Sanders have been making a few gigs together, and each man seems intent on getting the human voice and soul into his playing. In fact, Brown and Sanders, at Sanders' insistence, have been practicing Yoga breathing exercises in an attempt to bring more flesh into their sound. Brown told one citizen, "I want my horn to sound more and more like the human voice . . . pretty soon this instrument won't be an instrument anymore . . ." These men are pushing into newer areas of expression, and the work they have accomplished already, so far largely in semi-private due to the stupidity of the commercial record and nightclub industry, is intelligent and movingly beautiful.

Does anybody really think it's weird that all these English

"pop" groups are making large doses of loot? It's pretty simple, actually. They take the style (energy construct, general form, etc.) of black blues, country or city, and combine it with the visual image of white American non-conformity, i.e., the beatnik, and score very heavily. Plus the fact that these English boys are literally "hipper" than their white counterparts in the U.S., hipper because as it is readily seen, they have actually made a contemporary form, unlike most white U.S. "folk singers" who are content to imitate "ancient" blues forms and older singers, arriving at a kind of popular song (at its most hideous in groups like Peter, Paul and Mary, etc.), which has little to do with black reality, which would have been its strength anyway—that reference to a deeper emotional experience. As one young poet said, "At least The Rolling Stones come on like English crooks."

I say this as one way to get into another thing: namely, that even the avant-garde American music suffers when it moves too far from the blues experience. All the young players now should make sure they are listening to The Supremes, Dionne Warwick, Martha and The Vandellas, The Impressions, Mary Wells, James Brown, Major Lance, Marvin Gaye, Four Tops, Bobby Bland, etc., just to see where contemporary blues is; all the really nasty ideas are right there, and these young players are still connected with that reality, whether they understand why or not. Otherwise, jazz, no matter the intellectual bias, moved too far away from its most meaningful sources and resources is weakened and becomes, little by little, just the music of another emerging middle class. Forms become rigid when they come to exist only as ends, in themselves. That is, when they are seemingly autonomous (impossible, anyway, it's just that the content, then, is so weakened because all emphasis is on the form). What you say and how you say it are indissolubly connected . . . How *is* What. But too much attention to how will be performance in the dumbest *sense*. (Cents.)

Form is the structure of content. Right form is perfect expression of content.

*Would any musicians be willing to turn over to me all the information they have regarding the filthy cabaret card situation in New York City? Maybe we can get some of these graft-sucking creeps in trouble.*

# 1966

## Apple Cores #3

ALBERT AYLER is the dynamite sound of the time. He says he's not interested in note; he wants to play past note and get, then, purely into sound. Into the basic element, the clear emotional thing, freed absolutely from anti-emotional concept. The records have been beautiful, at first frightening, because they tear so completely away, are not at all "reasonable," i.e., have done away with the "explanation," the connection with the awe-inspiring popular song. When Ayler does want memory to furnish him with a fire source, he uses coonish churchified chuckle tunes. Deedee-dedaaa, going straight back to the American origins of African music. And all rhythmically oriented. The taps (vibrato) in his tone are rhythm hitches, and pump the melody into the pure rhythm part. When he uses drummer, Milford Graves, the backdrop is great natural roars and chugs and stops and puffs and scrambling. Graves weaves and wheels in the back, the sound always changing. Never the quickly dull pre-felt tapping of the simply hip. The sound and sound devices, always changing, and the energy pushing it, unflagging.

When Ayler uses Sonny Murray, the group has a completely different total sound. There are more things on Murray's mind, more sentimental precisions he tries to resolve like a violinist. Graves is more single minded in intent. He simply wants to go straight ahead. Murray sometimes makes you think he might just want to disappear.

Murray's "flying" style is visually as well as musically pro-
vocative. Sonny lunges and floats over the drums and cymbals striking, near-striking, brushing, missing, caressing all
the sound surfaces, while accompanying himself with a deep
wailing that cuts down deep into the flesh.

Murray's rhythmic reorganization makes the drums song-
ful. His accents are from immediate emotional necessity
rather than the sometimes hackneyed demands of a pre-
stated meter, in which one cymbal is beat on coyly in the
name of some fashionable soulforce.

The drums surprise and hide and are subtle, or suddenly
thunderous. In some passages Murray has both feet working,
straightout, and the drumsticks (which are metal tubes, or
knitting needles, even, sometimes, wood) are not even visible.

The drum "line" swoops is loud, is soft and sometimes
seems to disappear, as well. But it is a total drum music
Murray makes, not just ear-deafening "accompaniment."

A great many young and not so young drummers have
learned from Murray, especially during his work with the
Cecil Taylor unit. Sonny is coming into his own now. And his
weird graphic charts, some of which look like ingenious
machines, will probably be hot stuff in the next few seasons.

Don Ayler, Albert's younger brother, puts the style into
trumpet playing. He roars and goes straight through note to
wide-open horn sound. Don, now, has little respect for the
reflective, but by the nature of his playing, when he does
become more analytical, the long blasts will be in profound
black technicolor.

The group Ayler used several times at the Black Arts was
Don and Charles Tyler, a wild Ayler-like alto player, who is
also from Cleveland. Tyler is one of the best alto men on the
scene right now, and he's just starting. Ditto Don Ayler, on
his loud horn.

Other people are Milford Graves and bassist Louis Worrell, who both played with the John Tchicai-Roswell Rudd
group.

There was talk for a while about an Ayler group featuring both Graves and Sonny Murray. I hope it happens. Be completely out of sight. Graves the intelligent fist, Murray the mysticism. Ayler has both elements in his music.

The newest album Ayler has is *Bells*, on hip Bernard Stollman's ESP records. All the ESP records I've heard are worth having. I hope the musicians are benefiting as much from the recordings as the producer and the consumers. (A likely story.)

Another record out fairly recently of Ayler's that should be mentioned on every page of this jive magazine,* is *Spiritual Unity*, with Sonny Murray, and Gary Peacock on bass. Even you freaks with the paper ears should get this album, it might cool you out from hurting somebody!

More black music of our time. The Sun-Ra Myth-Science Arkestra. Sun-Ra has been on the general scene for a long time. In Chicago, quite a few years ago, I remember hearing the name and seeing a film *The Cry of Jazz*, in which Sun's music was featured.

All the concepts that seemed vague and unrealized in the late 50's have come together in the mature and profound music and compositions of this philosopher-musician.

The Arkestra varies in size. But it is usually about ten to twelve musicians large. Sometimes two drummers (e.g., Roger Blank and Clifford Jarvis or Jihmmie Johnson) plus all the other hornmen doubling on all kinds of percussion instruments ... bells, cymbals, African wood drums.

Sun-Ra wants a music that will reflect a life-sense lost in the West, a music full of Africa. The band produces an environment, with their music most of all, but also with their dress (gold cloth of velvet, headbands and hats, shining tunics). The lights go out on some tunes, and the only lights

* *Down Beat.*

are flashing off a band on Sun-Ra's head, or from altoist, Marshall Allen's, or some of the other sidemen.

On one piece, the Arkestra moves, behind Sun-Ra, in a long line through the dark, chanting and playing, with the lights flashing on and off . . . a totally different epoch is conjured.

The musicians also sing, on quite a few of the songs, e.g. "Next Stop, Jupiter," some of them pointing in the air. The voice becomes more and more relevant to contemporary jazz. From the vocal quality of the most impressive horns, to "A Love Supreme," or Archie Shepp's spoken "Malcolm," or Albert Ayler's short biographical talk on *My Name Is Albert Ayler*, or Sonny Murray's humming on "Witches and Devils" (ESP *Spiritual Unity*) or my own reading with John Tchicai.

Sun-Ra's new record for ESP *The Heliocentric World of Sun-Ra* is one of the most beautiful albums I have ever heard. It is a deeply filling experience. And one realization that this album gave me was the fact that the Sun-Ra Myth-Science Arkestra is really the first big band of the New Black Music. The Ornette Coleman Double Quartet, and the feel of the Cecil Taylor compositions on "Into the Hot" were my first references of what the new music's big bands would sound like. And Sun-Ra's manipulation of sound within this orchestral context is even more flexible in terms of spontaneous composition and the utilization of a "total sound" concept, i.e., when the music seems to take up all available sound space. Sun-Ra's music in this term presumes it exists everywhere. All Nature. And is not merely the calm artifact lost in a world of silence. The popular song is clearly discernable as a thing in the world. Its limits are blatantly finite. Sun-Ra's music creates the arbitrary sounds of the natural world.

Sun-Ra's Arkestra is really a black family. The leader keeps fourteen or fifteen musicians playing with him who are convinced that music is a priestly concern and a vitally significant aspect of black culture. Some of the musicians, like new tenor man John Gilmore or baritonist Pat Patrick, might have jobs with other bread bands, but their strongest dedication is to the beautiful black sound-world of Sun-Ra.

Most of the players in Sun-Ra's Myth-Science Arkestra are still too young to be known by more than a few people. But the *Heliocentric* album ought to change all that.

Impulse record release called *The New Wave in Jazz*, was supposed to be called "New Black Music" . . . it is a live concert at the Village Gate for the benefit of the Black Arts Repertory Theater School. Featured on the album are John Coltrane playing an amazing version of "Nature Boy," Archie Shepp's group, Albert Ayler quartet, Grachun Moncur and trumpeter Charlie Tolliver with a group made up of Charles Spaulding, Cecil McBee and Billy Higgins.

Two other groups were supposed to be recorded, Betty Carter, who really turned the place out, and Sun-Ra's huge band. But due to some weird twisting by the A&R man, two highlights of this really live concert were blanked out.

But this is the record to get. Trane, Ayler and Shepp, the big horns of our time, plus people like Bobby Hutcherson, Marion Brown, Pharoah Sanders, Sonny Murray, Don Ayler, Louis Worrell.

The Black Arts will be releasing a series of albums soon. The first side in the series is called *Sonny's Time Now*. Its drummer, Sonny Murray's first date as leader. Featured are Albert Ayler, Don Cherry and two bassists, Louis Worrell and Henry Grimes.

This album should really spring Murray loose. He's been out front for so long, it's time real light got focused on him. Perhaps the names of the tunes will give some idea of what the session was like. Three tunes; "Virtue," "Justice," "The Lie," as well as one tune called "Black Art." This album should turn everybody around. All the tunes are Murray's, and the last piece is poetry-jazz exploration.

Murray's drums are like strange pieces of sculpture, or at least the pieces he designs himself are. At this date, he had only two of his own cymbals. The ride cymbal hung from a wrought iron structure, and the highhats were anchored by a wire device between the two cymbals, which altered the rate and angle of contact.

Great White Liberals of The World, give all these young men a job, or at least some money! Until they learn, and all other black people learn, that they must finally support themselves.

# 1966

## Apple Cores #4

LAST NIGHT black genius ignited a cellar in Newark. The vibrations in the place were bad when I first got there. A kind of heavy neo-pseudo-black-white-gray bohemian thing hangs around like wet atmosphere in the *Hound of the Baskervilles*. All the sick grays hanging on the walls. A nothing trio of Red Garland, etc., imitators were playing. Plus some slick-haired gray poet gave me his booklet defending housing projects and CORE-integration. Dungeon electricity was probably what I was getting, and it turned me off, off.

Coming back from a juice run they were getting ready for another reading. This one by a poet named Ronald Stone, a brother whose name I'd heard with favorable reports. The reports are sound. This brother can wail. His poems got so much fire together three of the housing-project poet's audience split to "get back to their baby sitters." Really.

Stone reads into his work. He takes it and orchestrates it. Makes it music, and he is very conscious of the fact. Sometimes he uses songs, as quotes, as movements and springboards in the poem. One poem uses song titles, mostly jazz tunes, to make a hard lyric direction. He has love poems, too, turned very consciously by the woman thing. The black woman, i.e., how to get her back with us.

His work is funny, acid and moving. Sometimes he sings some of the lines (reminding you of Roland Snellings, Larry

Neal) or he can raise the words under a passion of almost rhetorical drama (vis-à-vis Calvin Hernton). But the final emotional totality is Stone's. His stone own.

Stone changed the whole tone of the evening. The vibrations got much better, the air a little clearer, the entire joint at least three or four aliens cooler.

Charles Moore, the young Detroit trumpet player did a short crackling set. He also played with the last group of the evening. This group, which was billed as The Detroit Artists' Workshop, really featured brilliant young New York musicians; Pharoah Sanders, Marion Brown and Rashid-Ali. The Detroiters, Moore, and the others were also joined by two local Newark players, altoist George Lyle and tenor man Howard Walker, who turned out to be smoking as well. But the whole set, I think it was two tunes, made for one of those very rare occasions when even the furniture seems to be moving. So fiery did the thing become.

At one point, with all the horns going off on their own, yet tied to the final movement and feeling of the whole, some of us in the audience were moaning and blowing with the players, and the music took us all, musicians and listeners, out past our eyes.

Sanders, his first ESP record notwithstanding, is a fantastic musician. (And even the ESP side, if you listen to what Pharoah is trying to do, where he's trying to go, even then, you'll get the point. But his sidemen on the side, especially Jane Getz, who keeps banging this one cripple chord on her insensitive box, like she's crying for lost Pharoah to come back to popular-song land, are no help at all.) His command of harmonics (three, four, ten notes at once), his lyric timbre even when he is screaming, his control of the horn with his breathing . . . whatever the "note value," enable him to play a long heroic line of moving richness.

Sanders was the mover of the evening. Though Brown, Ali and the others played as strong as they could, and all were visibly moved and shaken by the experience. At the height of the music, the moaning and screaming came on in earnest. This is the esctasy of the new music. At the point of wild agony or joy, the wild moans, screams, yells of life, in constant change.

(Listening to Sonny Murray, you can hear the primal needs of the new music. The heaviest emotional indentation it makes. From ghostly moans of spirit, let out full to the heroic marchspirituals and priestly celebrations of new blackness. I mention Sonny here—and Albert Ayler and Sun-Ra—because their music is closest to the actual soul-juice, cultural genius of the new black feeling. The tone their music takes is a clear emotional reading of where the new music is. And Pharoah, Marion, Charles Moore and the others got into it the other night. And sound ran through us like blood.)

With all the different horns making their own communal space, and Ali supplying the earth feeling, like the movement across it, the heavy shadows of things who fly . . . you could feel the complexity of life, and the simplicity. All the sounds combined to be the (one) sound of the world, and moving through space at thousands of miles an hour.

Marion Brown, sometime Archie Shepp's altoist, and drummer Raschid-Ali, who has also played with Archie, were both very very hot this evening, but it was Sanders who did the actual flying. But Ali and Brown are moving to become important musicians themselves, very important. Raschid has made so much progress since I heard him last year it's fantastic. And Brown, having played with Shepp, and shedded with Pharoah is moving, very quickly, as well. The only danger I can see that might hinder either of these strong players is a danger that is perhaps close to all the young rising players of the new music, i.e., the danger of becoming merely "stylists,"—hip reflectors of what's going on, rather than explorers, and more than that, finders and changers, which is, believe it or not, finally where it's at.

There was some newer talent on the scene as well. I mentioned Charles Moore, the young trumpet player from Detroit. Right now, he has the strongest sound on that horn, except for innovator Don Ayler. And Moore has probably heard Ayler, because that overpowering brass sound is something that Don has almost singlehandedly returned to jazz, under the influence of Albert Ayler's strong horn.

Moore is young and still, sometimes, wants to play "tunes," i.e., bits of memorablia, not strictly his own blood tone; but he is still way out there, and I would suppose, still moving.

Another young horn is altoist George Lyle, who has been turned around, it seems, by Ayler and Shepp. He has a fresh aggressive sound on alto, a horn which can sound like white squeaky ladies under the wrong heart. Post Ornette, now, the sound of the alto has to be worked on. Tchicai has the light, tight, sound; ditto, Marion Brown, Giuseppe Logan, etc., though Marshall Allen, Sun-Ra's main altoist, has a bigger prettier sound. Only Charles Tyler of the Ayler unit has the big wailing heavy alto sound that satisfies my particular need for flesh and blood. The Jackie McLean-Ornette Coleman "broad" alto sound is something to be picked upon by the younger players. Lyle sounds right now like he might be thinking about it.

# 1966

## Apple Cores #5—
## The Burton Greene Affair

THE QUALITY of being is what soul is, or what a soul is. What is the quality of your being? Quality here meaning, what does it possess? What a being doesn't possess, by default, also determines the quality of the being—what its soul actually is.

And let us think of soul, as *anima:* spirit (*spiritus,* breath) as that which carries breath or the living wind. We are animate because we breathe. And the spirit which breathes in us, which animates us, which drives us, makes the paths by which we go along our way and is the final characterization of our lives. Essence/Spirit. The final sum of what we call being, and the most elemental. There is no life without spirit. The human being cannot exist without a soul, unless the thing be from evil-smelling freezing caves breathing high-valence poison gases now internalized into the argon-blue eyes.

What your spirit is is what you are, what you breathe upon your fellows. Your internal and elemental volition.

At the *Jazz Art Music Society* in Newark, one night, pianist Burton Greene performed in a group made up of Marion Brown, alto saxophone and Pharoah Sanders, tenor saxophone.

Greene's performance, strange as it was, was not really unique. Its meanings were the way the world always speaks. "Existence proves itself."

I want here to list some observations I made of the existence of soul and anti-soul or the spiritual and the anti-spiritual . . . how they do exist.

The Burton Greene Affair, I have called it because Burton Greene is a white, super-hip (MoDErN) pianist whose work is and will be praised and soon raised when Morgenstern and Company become his Joshuas and the walls of the banks fall down.

The music this night was rising and grew heavy beating the walls of that place. A trembling music . . . especially that Pharoah Sanders makes with his long harmonics-driven line (Nazakat Ali and Salamat Ali from Pakistan can do this with their voices). Marion Brown was rising with Pharoah. It was a mad body-dissolving music . . . rose and stayed there . . . ecstasy of understanding then, evolution. The feeling such men make is of the consciousness of evolution, the *will* of the universe.

Yes, it is music which, under the best fingers, is a consciously Spiritual Music. That is, we mean to speak of Life Force and try to *become* one of the creative functions of the universe.

So Sun-Ra, who knows something of the Wisdom Religion itself, uses this knowledge to make his music bridge to higher human principles. Sun-Ra speaks of the actual change, the actual evolution through space, not only in space ships, but of the higher principles of humanity, the *progress* after the death of the body.

Pharoah Sanders is a spiritual person. He also wants to feel the East, as an oriental man. Marion Brown wants to understand what spiritual is, and he follows and associates with certain spiritual energies. That is, he understands it is, to a certain extent, about energy.

To be spiritual is to be in touch with the living magnetism of life-world-universe. "All you folks got rhythm!" Right! (And it is harder for a rich man to enter the kingdom of heaven, etc., etc.) Rich to mean *perverted by things*, which is America, the occident. Where the sun dies.

In the beautiful writhe of the black spirit-energy sound the whole cellar was possessed and animated. Things flew through the air.

Burton Greene, at one point, began to bang aimlessly at the keyboard. He was writhing, too, pushed by forces he could not use or properly assimilate. He kept running his fingers compulsively through his hair.

Finally he stood above the piano . . . the music around him flying . . . and began to strike the piano strings with his fingers and knock on the wood of the instrument. He got a drumstick to make it louder. (Greene's "style" is pointed, I would presume, in the direction of Cecil Taylor, and I would also suppose, with Taylor the Euro-American Tudor-Cage, Stockhausen-Wolf-Cowell-Feldman interpretations.)

But the sound he made would not do, was not where the other sound was. He beat the piano, began to slam it open and shut slapping the front and side and top of the box. The sound would not do, would not be what the other sound was.

He sat again and doodled, he slumped his head. He ran his fingers desultorily across the keys. Pharoah and Marion still surged; they still went on screaming us into spirit.

Burton Greene got up again. A sudden burst like at an offending organism he struck out again at the piano . . . he beat and slammed and pummeled it. (The wood.) He hit it with his fist.

Finally he sprawled on the floor, under the piano, shadow knocking on the piano bottom, on his elbows he tapped, tapped furiously then subsided to a soft flap, bap bap then to silence, he slumped to quiet his head under his arm and the shadow of the piano.

Pharoah and Marion were still blowing. The beautiful sound went on and on.

# 1966

## Apple Cores #6

Don Pullen-Milford Graves *Live at Yale University:*\*
    "This record is part of our self-reliance program for
    musicians,"
is on a piece of news print printed in red. With the title. DP
Piano, MG percussion. The album cover is hand painted.
Delicate forms in blue, green, orangish-yellow white. A
blown landscape of event.

THE MUSIC IS beautiful on this album. And the idea of its
distribution—do it yourself, brother. Not brother can you
spare a 10 percent. Do it yourself, in nations, cultures, products of the mind and soul. Visions. Your own, yourself and
the other kindred selves. The music is beautiful on this
album.

You know that we do not have one theater of our own . . .
where are the jazz record companies? . . . Motown should
show you what you can do if you got a gut product. The
music is beautiful.

Sun-Ra has been doing this for years. His self. Saturn
hovers above all of us. Sun-Ra, who is the modern master.
The orchestrator.

On this record, Don Pullen shows how deeply he has

---

\* Don Pullen-Milford Graves *In Concert at Yale University* (Pullen-Graves
Music).

stuck his exploding fingers. His piano is similar to Cecil Taylor's except Pullen is *heavier*, in the sense of carrying, perhaps, a thicker trunk. His piano waves a massier, more massive staff, hence it, his "line," seems slower, like a heavy waving carrying more harmonic implications than Cecil's. Cecil wants the quicker rhythmic change, the supra-physical tap-dance. Cecil seems "quicker," the changes. But Pullen's is a deep deep dreamlike "funk" (more toward meta than supra) in the mood of something always ominous wanting out, and getting it. And a kind of endlessness (variations on ommmmmmmmmmm) peeking out of behind everywhere. Pullen's music is beautiful. He is the strongest pianist in "Cecil's direction" I've heard, with something personal calling. And without, it would seem, that paranoid respect for "charts."

Milford Graves, with Pullen, sounds like some kind of natural phenomenon. Like marveling at thunder's pitch and dynamics. He fills all the spaces with movement, change of direction. Time is simply *occurrence*. It happened while, if you were, measuring. Can evolutionary processes, the constants, be said to march? The tap you hear is your own pulse, fellow being.

Do he swing?

Do anything?

This entire side (PG1 and PG2,) I suppose this title(s) along with the "Nothing"(s) on Milford's solo album *You Never Heard Such Sounds In Your Life* (ESP) are in the spirit of sensing the wholeness, the total involved in each experience. Names are different bits of a whole.

These two players, Pullen and Graves, are making some of the deepest music anywhere. It wants nothing.

Elsewhere, I've heard the second version of Coltrane's *Ascension.* I think the second version, which they are putting into the same jackets as the first, and generally not hip-

ping people to the switch, is superior. Or, it is a more grati-
fying experience. Especially as Pharoah Sanders' horn is
heard more clearly in something approaching its full
strength (on records). Trane's *Meditations* is, finally,
purer. There is an older Trane, his maturity, I've said before,
swanlike, his feeling for what was called pastoral, which we
know now to be the calmness of objective life. What it really
is, actually without incident. Trane's Ballad Form, ("Love")
he uses to spring the wild, exhausting sections ("Consequences" and the Ayler-like "The Father, The Son, The Holy
Ghost"), Pharoah Sanders really reaching his peak on these
tunes, especially "Consequences."

The wide-open ensembles, the working friezes . . . the
attempt at *total* definition are exciting and beautiful. It all
works. The whole music seems less "bound" (by charts, by
reading, by contracts, by spurious attentions) than before.
Pharoah's strength in this undertaking is unmistakable, and
the direction it is giving John's music. The *Meditations*
band brings Trane back to absolute contemporary expression, though Trane himself, it would seem, is content to
"scream" less, and prefers the older rhythmic feeling and his
gorgeous lyric sweep, anyway. I would like to hear Trane
come full out, as flag for the heavy Pharoah. Then the music
would reach still another level. Right now Pharoah is doing
the pumping.

I saw one of the Love Beast concerts; a name, I think, that
is fully appropriate. The Beast making money, using energy.
Some dazed "adventurers" licking on some of the wheres?

Sun-Ra, naturally, could not be included in a series of
concerts called Love Beast. The purity of the Sun God's
music could not be used, so it was not. And since Cecil
Taylor was not gotten to play, they did not even get to that
. . . that thing they say they want. The avant-garde, which

finally be, in their measure, bullshit, anyway, and a con-
glomerate of freaks, superfreaks, inferior freaks, an a lil'
white man off in the shadders collec'n duh gol'.

ART!

CREEPS!

Speaking of those two subjects, Frank Smith thinks he is
an Albert Ayler replica. (In a red shirt with all his other
boys, in blue suits, giving up ergs of energy to the guy in the
red shirt, and finally $$$$, since ol' Smitty will make it, like
jazz, all the way up the river to the offices of Henry Loose.)

Frank Smith is a kind of petty thief, except that what he
steals is not petty. He is the *Soul Thief*. He hovers in the
background with a red straw covered with hair for sticking
in people's haids sucking out the brains. He hunches over
when he plays like garbage falling. He blows what he heard
Albert blow. He is slick as a bat whistle.

But, lovers of cold fact, Mr. Smith will get rich, just as
soon as Albert's sound becomes understood by one stretch
this other layer of life will use the superslicksterized version
of it, Sir Smith, to prove how hip the missionaries always
are. And it's because that's what they wanted to hear, anyway,
themselves. (I kept thinking of Kate Smith, going crazy.)

This last item, is a found object:

Owner and Slave

If there were more Woody Hermans
and fewer or no Archie Shepps, the state
of Jazz would be much healthier

—Dave Yost
Spokane, Washington

"We try to use all components of music," Lloyd explained.

"Chordal composition and improvisation are not finished, *nor is complete freedom the answer.*"

here are some of the idiots floating around America
—Down Beat magazine July 16, 1966

# 1965

## New Tenor Archie Shepp Talking

HAVING TO CALL Archie Shepp a "new" tenor man on the scene is just one way of admitting the cultural lag between what any younger artist is doing, and the time it will take for the word to spread to the larger majority of jazz listeners. But Archie Shepp moved to New York's Lower East Side about five years ago, and he has been strongly in evidence ever since. (It seems also that the Lower East Side has become the holdout stomp grounds of a great many younger musicians, just as it has replaced Greenwich Village as a place where a great many poets, painters, etc., hole up because of cheaper rents and the presence of empathetic types.)

I first heard Archie Shepp when he was playing with Cecil Taylor's unit in Jack Gelber's play *The Connection*. What Shepp was playing that first night I heard him startled me (the word was, at the time, ". . . man, that cat'll scare you to death"), and what he has gotten into since has more than borne out my initial reaction, which was that we had just heard one of the most singular reed voices to come along in quite some time.

Quite a few people hear "a new wave Ben Webster," to quote one pundit, when listening to Archie. Quite a few others hear a strong Sonny Rollins influence; still others hear John Coltrane's presence in the Shepp approach to tenor saxophone playing. But what these people are really hearing is a young musician whose emotional registrations are so broad that he is able, quite literally, to make reference to anybody's "style," even though finally all the ideas and images that make his playing so beautiful seem completely his own. That's another big drag about this cultural lag business, there are people always comparing these young musicians to someone else, etc. even long after the musician has gotten off into his own thing. I mean, you listen to Archie Shepp, and the only real influences you can admit are "everything." Artists are influenced, finally, by everything. Listening to Archie Shepp talk about his music and his life will convince you even further about the autonomy of his ideas and musical direction.

"I was born in Fort Lauderdale, Florida, in 1937 . . . we lived there about seven years, then moved to Philly, where I lived most of my life. I started playing when I was about fifteen years old. My aunt got me a saxophone . . . she had had no children of her own. I had had a clarinet a few years before, an old silver horn. We also had an old old upright for as long as I was home. My father was an old banjo player from the old days. He used to play in Florida with a few groups. One group he played with was led by a cat named Hartley Toots . . . he was the wizard of the banjo in south Florida. He was my father's teacher. They played all over Florida.

"We lived in the Germantown area of Philly, which was mostly a white bourgeois area, but there were these pocket ghettoes like the one we used to live in, right there among the whites. They called the ghetto I lived in 'The Brickyard.' So I got a chance to go to Germantown High, which was a pretty good school. They usually tried to funnel the Negro students out of there into Gratz and Gillespie in the larger Negro areas. But there were some guys playing at the high school I went to.

"Mastbaum was the school, though . . . that's where there were a whole lot of cats playing . . . that's North Philly. Most of the cats lived further south in North Philly. Everybody was trying to get that early Jazz Messenger sound then. Lee Morgan and a alto player named Kenny Rogers really got me started playing jazz. Kenny first recorded with Lee . . . he used to sound like early Lou Donaldson . . . you know, that great big alto sound.

"There was a place called the Jazz Workshop run by a disc jockey I used to go to after school. I guess that was the place where I really began to hear jazz, I mean really hear it. Before that I just heard my father, mostly Dixieland and R&B. Lee frequented the place all the time . . . he and Kenny were like local heroes, and this was about the time Lee was fourteen. He was a very young cat, but he was playing. Henry Grimes, Ted Curson, Bobby Timmons used to come in too. There was something like a rivalry between the North Philly and South Philly musicians. Spanky De Brest was from North Philly. It seemed like some very good bass players came out of South Philly, like Jimmy Garrison and Grimes. South Philly was the original Negro settlement, but the flux had been to the north.

"At the Workshop they'd have people like Chet Baker and Russ Freeman as the main group, but after they'd get finished they let the young cats come on and play. I started talking to Lee at this place one time and went home with him and Kenny. They asked me who I liked . . . I said Brubeck and Getz. And they really wigged out . . . but they were being very very hip. I was square as a mf. You can imagine the reaction. They said, Oh yeah? So then these cats asked me to take out my horn and play something. I had a C Melody sax about that time, and I guess I had a sort of Stan Getz sound. Print that laugh! Lee was doing everything he could to keep from laughing in my face. But then he pulled out his horn and played the blues with me. The blues was

something I'd been playing for a long time, because of my
old man. I heard a lot of the blues then . . . I had to forget all
about my Stan Getz shit. Then I just played like I play . . . I
didn't know any chord changes at all but I could hear the
blues . . . I could always hear the blues. So then these cats
stopped playing and said Yeah, that was right. Then after
that, they sort of took an interest in me. It was my introduction to real jazz music.

"Another important introduction to jazz was hearing Bird
at a concert one night. He was playing at this concert opposite a thirty-nine piece band led by an arranger named Herb
Gordy (Oscar Pettiford, Red Rodney, Don Elliot, Terry
Gibbs were in the big band). Nobody thought Bird would
show up, cause he didn't have a horn, but somehow he managed. But strangely, I had seen the cat earlier that day on
Girard Street, although I didn't know it was him. But I saw
this cat on Girard Street in a wrinkled dirty blue vine with a
fine looking blonde on his arm. Chan? I'd never seen a black
man with a white woman. And when I did I thought he'd
be clean, but this cat struck me. He was raggety as a mf. He
was just walking around, on his way to the concert. He
walked in with the chick, and played his ass off. Later on he
got Red Rodney from the other group to play with him . . .
and they really played."

During high school there were the inevitable rhythm gigs
which have served to keep so many young jazz players alive
and also, I believe, given them a strong blues foundation to
work from. Archie played with a R&B group with Lee Morgan and Kenny Rogers around Philadelphia called Carl
Rogers and His Jolly Stompers. "Lee turned me on to
changes . . . I had learned them, but I didn't know how to
use them. Lee and Kenny helped me find out how to use
changes rhythmically."

After high school the hand of liberal America took hold of
Archie as "the Negro" they wanted to see go to a "progres-

sive" college. "I wanted to go to college, but my parents sure couldn't send me. I applied to Lincoln University and could have gotten a partial scholarship . . . but then this college in Vermont, Goddard, put out the word that they were looking for a Negro student, to give a full scholarship to. Goddard's a progressive school on the order of Bard or one of those. So I went up there and majored in dramatic literature.

"I wasn't playing as much in college as I had been, but I kept at it. Originally I'd planned on taking law in school, but I came under the influence of one of the drama coaches at the school. He read a story I did for English class, and he said he was impressed by it . . . that it was like a play. He wanted to know had I ever thought about writing plays. Finally, I changed my major. Yeh, my parents were pretty upset about my going into such a nebulous field. You know, it was the old story . . . people saying anything in the arts is good for a hobby, but you can't make a dollar. But I will say that it was at Goddard that I first got interested in sociopolitical activity." And Archie Shepp is one of the most engagé of jazz musicians old or young. He is critically aware of the social responsibility of the black artist, which, as quiet as it's kept, helps set one's aesthetic stance as well. In this sense, ethics and aesthetics, as Wittgenstein said, are one.

Archie stayed at Goddard until 1959 when he was graduated. When he came out of school he came straight to New York. "I first came into New York in 1957, during what they called the winter work term. I was living with an aunt in Harlem, rather than go back to Philly. In 1959 I moved to the Lower East Side and married a girl I'd met in school in 1958. John Coltrane was the first real influence on my playing. I never heard him in Philly, I knew of him. There was a bitch of a tenor player in Philly, Lee Grimes, who went insane. Well, Lee was influenced by Trane when it wasn't fashionable. Lee was the first person I heard playing harmonics, and because I was raving about him, someone said I ought to hear Coltrane. But I didn't until college. I dug him immediately.

"When I came to New York I'd go down to the Five Spot where he was playing. One night I just went up to him and told him I was from Philly and would sure appreciate talking to him. I went up to see him in a few days, and he took a lot of time with me. He was very courteous and obliging. It was the first time a man, a musician, who was really out there, who knew a lot, had ever taken any time with me. I was playing alto then. I had had this tenor I told you about . . . that my aunt gave me. But somehow I never felt satisfied. Somebody told me that Jimmy Heath (who by the way I have a lot of respect for) and Trane played alto first . . . before they played tenor. So I decided to get an alto. I took this brand new Martin that my aunt gave me to the shop, and the cat there gave me an old antique alto in trade. My folks almost went out of their minds. I'd traded a three hundred dollar horn for a twenty dollar one. And that was my lot, as far as horns went until 1960 when I was with Cecil Taylor. After I met Trane I got a second-hand tenor.

"I went to Florida in 1960 and played a lot of rock and roll gigs down there. When I got back to New York I started going down to the Cafe Wha? in the Village, Don Ellis and Dave Pike were playing down there. I met Buell Neidlinger and Billy Osborn down there, too. Buell had already been playing with Cecil, and Buell and Billy used to persuade Dave Pike to let me sit in. I'd bring my horn and wait for those cats to come in.

"Buell had told Cecil about me I guess, and one day he came in and the two of them played. After a few weeks I met Cecil and he said he was looking for me . . . he was doing a record for Candid, and he wanted me on it. I started going down to Cecil's pad . . . I didn't know what the cat was doing . . . even when we did the record I was a bit confused. But I started going down to his pad, and we used to play, just me and him. Sonny Murray (Taylor's drummer for quite a few years, now working with Albert Ayler, Don Cherry and Gary Peacock in Europe)* was living in the next apartment and he used to come in and play. It took me from then . . . about 1961 through 1962 to begin to get an idea of what was going on . . . so that I really knew . . . I got to a point where I thought I did know . . . but I couldn't say what was happening . . . but I felt the music. By the time we made that record for Impulse *Into the Hot* I had gotten pretty familiar with what was happening . . . It was one of the most valuable musical experiences I've had. The things that Trane told me sufficed up until the time I met Taylor, and that's what projected me into what I'm doing now."

And Archie has come quite a way since his first days with Cecil Taylor. Now the sound is larger, even more overpowering, the ideas fluid, and the energy stirs up spirits everywhere. With groups like The New York Contemporary Five, which was Don Cherry, John Tchicai, J. C. Moses and Don Moore, or recording groups like the one he used on the soon to be released *Four for Trane* . . . Tchicai; Roswell Rudd; young trumpeter, Allen Shorter; Reggie Workman, Archie has moved right into the front line of tenor saxophonists of any persuasion. But the influence of Cecil Taylor's ideas on Shepp's playing is still very evident, as far as Shepp's insistence that melody must be natural, i.e., projected out of the rhythm core of the music. And Archie has one of the most melodic horn lines around, like someone said recently of his work at a party, "That cat plays just like he was singing."

Of Cecil Taylor: "Cecil has dispensed with a harmonic base, to a large extent. Before I worked with Cecil, I used to listen for chords. When I was playing with the group in *The Connection* I played a lot of Cecil's tunes. He'd play these

---

* In a group fronted by Albert Ayler.

things with a lot of clusters . . . I mean you could interpret these as maybe a C, C-sharp, D, D-sharp, E and F, or C7th, C-sharp 7th, D7th, D-sharp 7th, E or F . . . it was really up for grabs, and for a while a cat could go crazy wondering, which chord should you play at this point. Very often in his compositions, when Cecil would be working with harmonically oriented musicians, he'd have chords written out, but they'd change every two beats and if the tempo was way up it'd be impossible to play them. I'd take them home and try to play them, and it sounded like I was doing exercises . . . then, finally, I got to a point where I thought maybe these chords might not be absolutely necessary.

"Cecil plays lines . . . something like a row or scale . . . that lends itself to the melodic shape of the tune, which is derived from the melody, so that the harmony many times becomes subservient to the body of the tune. And the chords he plays are basically percussive.

"But playing with Taylor, I began to be liberated from thinking about chords. I'd come back from Florida not sure what I wanted to do. I was in a quandary. I'd been imitating John Coltrane unsuccessfully, and because of that I was really chord conscious. At first it didn't seem like a liberation . . . it was frightening. It called the whole foundation of what I knew into question. But then I became very conscious of the rhythm section. I hadn't thought too much about it before, with just that steady pulse. But with Cecil, because there's no steady pulse going, you have to be really conscious of what's going on rhythmically. Cecil plays the piano like a drum, he gets rhythms out of it like a drum, rhythm and melody. And this new music is about a melodic and rhythmic approach to the music. In a way it's more of a throwback rather than a projection into some weird future. A throwback in the direction of the African influences on the music.

"When black people first came to these shores they didn't know much harmony . . . that's a Western musical phenomenon. But they had melodies and tremendous rhythms. Spirituals were not that involved harmonically. 'Sometimes I Feel Like a Motherless Child' . . . I doubt that they were even thinking of harmony when they invented the melody, and the melody line is fantastic. The new music reaches back to the roots of what jazz was originally. In a way it's a rebellion against the ultrasophistication of jazz. Bird took harmony as far as it could go. Trane, too. But now Trane seems to be going into a thing that's aharmonic, totally melodic . . . and Elvin, the rhythm, playing all the time. Rhythm and melody. It's what Ornette and Cecil are into already.

"It's ironic about Cecil that he's a pianist and the piano is a harmonic instrument . . . you think of a piano player playing harmony, chords, and Cecil plays some, but he plays rhythm, in an almost basic, primitive concept of piano . . . striking it like a drum. Working with him I became aware of the function of rhythm and melody. And when I left I had a fairly clear idea who I was on my instrument. There wasn't anybody around at the time to imitate on a saxophone playing this kind of music, except Ornette. It was like a pioneer field.

"The reason Ornette wasn't such a big influence on me was because when I first heard him I wasn't prepared to listen . . . there was nothing wrong with his music . . . there was something wrong with my listening. After Cecil, I dug Ornette because I'd grown musically. People say Ornette sounds like Bird, but I don't think so . . . and even if there is something of Bird in his playing he's gotten way past it. He has a highly individual sound . . . Albert Ayler gets a highly individual sound, too.

"People also say I sound like Ben Webster or Lucky Thompson . . . well, there's so much to learn by listening to those people, but also there's so much room to take this sound and do something else with it, not better, but different, there are so many possibilities in music. Cecil freed me from the doldrums . . . I thought I'd heard all that jazz could do . . . it was like a door being opened to go into something else. Many people don't like our music because it's not conventional . . . the jazz audience is still in the process of development. The people in Europe are at a post-Bird stage . . . they're about up to Coltrane. But we still found an audience for the kind of music we (New York Contemporary Five) were playing."

(Archie in the black loft world is something again. He stands up very strong looking, bulky, his head thrown back just far enough to look movingly haughty. And all that strength, I mean what that environment demands—as for instance, at a weird Halloween party, with costumed realities disguised as their bags, and all the bunches of hard cats who don't wanna hear no bullshit—Archie, and all the other musicians there—Rudd, the exciting new drummer Milford Graves . . . get to this cat as soon as possible, he's scorching . . . bassist Louis Worrell, wanderer J. C. Moses sitting in long periods . . . scaring one little white girl into a domestic crisis . . . John Tchicai playing the alto like a metal poem, Charles Moffett and his wild drum and bugle corp rumble, Ornette Coleman, Cecil Taylor in the "audience," and all kinds of other innovators silent or loud—in that kind of environment, which no club can propose . . . e.g., "Where's them James Cagney Cigarettes?" . . . and with no other "reason" for being there but for the music, and if that's what they do think about, then everybody's in danger, because the music, then, is like they say very, very, tough, and you have to be tough to stand up under it. Archie can play, in these situations, and play his whole soul.)

Archie expressed the weight of black in his thinking, which is also, of course, in his playing: "The Negro musician is a reflection of the Negro people as a social and cultural phenomenon. His purpose ought to be to liberate America aesthetically and socially from its inhumanity. The inhumanity of the white American to the black American as well as the inhumanity of the white American to the white American is not basic to America and can be exorcised, gotten out. I think the Negro people through the force of their struggles are the only hope of saving America, the political or the cultural America.

"Culturally, America is a backward country, Americans are backward. But jazz is American reality. Total reality. The jazz musician is like a reporter, an aesthetic journalist of America. Those white people who used to go to those bistros in New Orleans, etc., thought they were listening to nigger music, but they weren't, they were listening to American music. But they didn't know it. Even today those white people who go slumming on the Lower East Side may not know it but they are listening to American music . . . the Negro's contribution, his gift to America. Some whites seem to think they have a right to jazz . . . perhaps that's true . . . but they should feel thankful for jazz . . . it has been a gift that the Negro has given, but they can't accept that, there are too many problems involved with the social and historical relationship of the two peoples. It makes it difficult for them to accept jazz and the Negro as its true innovator.

"So far I don't think the majority of white jazz musicians realize their function in jazz. They haven't found what their true roots are, they haven't dared go back to their own roots. I read an article by Lennie Tristano in *Down Beat* where he made some grievous statements, very shocking, almost racist, if I can use that word. It was a statement like, 'just because a Negro plays jazz it doesn't necessarily make him a man.' Well that's a gratuitous assumption on his part; I don't think every Negro feels that way, maybe some . . . I know about the cult of soul and that shit . . . but for a man to have that much gall, especially a white man, playing a music which has been given to him, rather graciously . . . in the light of that oppression . . . I think that man should be rather careful with his words, especially when he's criticizing the giver of a gift, you dig?—a marvelous gift."

# 1965

## Four for Trane

*Four for Trane*\* Impulse A-71
Archie Shepp, tenor; John Tchicai, alto; Roswell Rudd,
trombone; Allen Shorter, trumpet; Reggie Workman, bass;
Charles Moffet, drums.

|          (1)          |          (2)          |
|-----------------------|-----------------------|
| "Syeeda's Song Flute" | "Cousin Mary"         |
| "Mr. Syms"            | "Niema"               |
|                       | "Rufus" (swung his face at last to the wind, and then his neck snapped) |

Recorded Aug. 10, 1964

IT SEEMS an intolerably long time to me, since I first heard
of Archie Shepp, heard him play, until right now when Impulse is finally getting around to giving Archie an entire
record date with himself as leader. Archie made one record
before as co-leader with trumpeter Bill Dixon, and he has
also shared a record with Dixon, each man leading separate
groups on one half of an LP.

Why it has been so long, or seems so long, is not so hard to

\* Liner notes for *Four for Trane* (Impulse A-71)
   © 1965 by ABC Records, Inc.
   1330 Avenue of the Americas
   New York, New York 10019
All Rights Reserved. Used by Permission.

understand. Even though there are tons of LPs coming out monthly that all seem tailored for Lyndon Johnson, there are very few that feature musicians who have something new, strong and completely their own to say. Cecil Taylor, for instance, still only manages to record now and again, and not with any regularity at all, even though he is one of the most important musical influences of our time. Ditto, Ornette Coleman, another giant, who is now not recording at all, due to the churlishness and fanatic bad taste of most of the people in the music *business*. But this is a hopeless wailing on my part, I suppose, since most artists . . . painters, poets, musicians, etc. . . . are just about all ways subject and subjected to the whims and stiff inflexibility of the business heads who control the art "game." So there's no real need to go off into all that since most people with any kind of sense know, for certain, that the American business man, of whatever persuasion, is apt to be, at best, embarrassing in his limitations.

Listening to this album, *Four for Trane*, (Impulse A-71) one can see what we are being deprived of by just such menace as I mentioned above. This group that Shepp has gotten together for this date cannot fail to delight and inspire anyone really interested in moving human expression. First of all, Archie Shepp has risen very quickly, in my estimation, to the first rank of "post-Trane" tenor players. And I think the fact that this album is called *Four for Trane* demonstrates how much of an emotional allegiance Shepp feels he owes John Coltrane. But even with such acknowledged "allegiance," don't think for a moment that you're going to hear J.C. played back at you intact. Archie is so much his own self that it is finally impossible to name one influence as having been the guiding one. Whole lots of people say they hear Ben Webster, others Sonny Rollins. But the weird lovely thing is that they are really hearing Archie Shepp, and his range of expression is so broad that he seems to take

in or to have digested most of the ways of playing tenor
saxophone, specific "schools" having really not much to do
with it. Archie is playing himself, like many of the other
younger musicians around these days, a great many of whom
have been moved by Ornette Coleman and Cecil Taylor to
investigate deeper wellsprings of emotion, and have come up
singing their own songs. Listen to Archie, for example, on
Roswell Rudd's arrangement of Trane's "Niema," and you'll
see immediately what I mean.

The group that Archie has gathered here for his first major
session is really impressive. John Tchicai is the young Negro
alto player from Denmark who played with Shepp's (and
Don Cherry's) New York Contemporary Five when they
were in Europe a year or so ago. Like Shepp, Tchicai carries
the world-spirit in his playing, what is happening now, to *all
of us,* whether we are sensitive enough to realize it or not.
Contemporary means that; with the feeling that animates
our time. Shepp, Tchicai and the other players on this album
do just that.

Trumpeter Allen Shorter, is also moving and playing with
a great deal of strength and beauty. His short sharp staccato
bursts and spikes of brass sound make your flesh respond
("Syeeda," "Mr. Syms"), like it's actually sound that's coming at you, sound and feeling. And Shorter is just beginning
to get to himself now, with this recording. There should be
no doubt, after hearing him on this album, that he is on his
way, on out.

Roswell Rudd, 1963 *Down Beat* International Critics'
New Star on trombone, is both a gifted arranger and exciting
instrumentalist. His arrangement of "Niema" should prove
that to anyone. This piece is so much like a concerto for
Archie and ensemble, reminding one of Duke's "impressionistic" masterpieces, say "Transbluesency" or "Chelsea
Bridge."

Charles Moffett and Reggie Workman should be more familiar names. Moffett was Ornette Coleman's drummer during the last public phase of Ornette's playing. His work can really be heard to good advantage here ("Rufus"), heavy, precise, driving the beat. Moffett also led one of the best young groups around New York earlier this year, featuring Shorter, Carla Bley on piano and a beautiful young tenor man from Little Rock, Pharoah Sanders.

Reggie Workman was Art Blakey's bassist for the last couple of years, but at this writing he is working with Albert "Tootie" Heath's trio (with Cedar Walton) at New York's Five Spot. On this album, however, you will hear a Reggie Workman that you might not have expected to hear. Strong as usual, but with a flexibility of rhythmic phrasing ("Rufus" and "Syeeda"!!) that makes you rehear his playing, as if for the first time.

The four Trane tunes rendered here are also played with such freshness that it makes you rehear them. "Syeeda's Song Flute," for instance, which I'd thought Trane had fixed for me for all time on *Giant Steps*, is here, totally revived. Roswell Rudd is especially a pleasure on this, with his big muscular trombone sound. The horn sounds, for a change, like there's a human agency behind it. Rudd, Grachan Moncur, Garnett Brown, Bernard McKinney, and Ali Hassan are a few musicians trying to restore some humanity to that horn, instead of, say, continuing to imitate J.J.'s automatons.

"Syeeda" is given a bigger feeling here, with Archie's impeccable arranging of the head; and the head functions here the way any written music ought to, to set the mood, the initial mode, of engagement (attack). Music, otherwise, should be arbitrary (as anything else), i.e., it should reflect only its player (maker). "Syeeda's" head (Trane's "tune") proposes one direction, more or less specific: it produces an image, feeling, sense function . . . extending . . . to where? (As the hard blues "Cousin Mary" also proposes another direction, equally specific, that is to be dealt with *arbitrar-*

*ily.*) To wherever you (the musician) can hear to go. Pulse
set up, then released. "Let me go" . . . on out. Then we listen
to what the soloist thinks . . . has reacted to . . . as (art)
function.

John Tchicai's solo on "Rufus" comes back to me again. It
slides away from the proposed. He is so precise and exact in
his registrations. Or his beautiful tenderness and clarity on
"Cousin Mary," which he turns completely around with his
solo, so that Mary has a lot more on her mind than wiggling
her hips, though, to be sure, she's still doing that too.

Archie comes in on "Syeeda" singing, almost, to himself.
But his playing possesses a wailing, crying feeling, like some
lyrical banshee, full of everything the blues has always
meant. But it is a very personal blues. The wild interplay
between Shepp and Rudd on this tune, underscored and
driven deeper into us by Moffett and Workman, is alone
worth the price of this album.

But Archie's tune "Rufus" moved me most (although they
are all so good, so deep, so satisfying). "Rufus" makes its
"changes" faster. *Changes* here meaning, as younger musicians use that word to mean "modulations," what I mean
when I say *image*. They change very quickly. The mind,
moving. Where R&B repeats its term over and over—even
beautiful R&B or blues, or the uses made of these forms by
our contemporary mainstream, are repetitious, though not
necessarily boringly so—this music accepts repetition as an
already accepted fact of life. You breathe, your heart beats,
quickens with the music's pulse, and yours . . . your foot
pats, these are the things we don't even think about. The
point then is to *move* it away from what we already know,
toward, into, what we only *sense*. Music is for the senses.
Music should make you *feel*. But, finally, unless you strip
yourself of outside interference, almost all your reactions
will be *social*. (Like a man who digs Mozart because it is
"high class," dig it?) But the point of living seems to me to

get to your actual feelings, as, say, these musicians want always to get to theirs. If you can find out who you are (you're no thing), then you can find out what you feel. Because we *are* our feelings, or our lack of them.

The music, possible feeling, is here. Where ever you are. All you have to do is listen. Listen!

# 1963

## Don Cherry

DON CHERRY was winner as New Star trumpeter, in the *Down Beat* critics' poll. Of course this will not help him find more work, now that he is no longer with the Sonny Rollins band (Sonny having decided that some ca. 1950 "hip" chords behind him and the absence of a "competing" solo voice, would make his own music sound better). Winning such an award would help Cherry find work if he *also* wanted to play like Miles Davis, etc., or at least said he did, or at least could spin a bass on his head while holding a note (as Roland Kirk did recently at the Village Gate). But, unfortunately, all Cherry's got going for him is his extraordinary musical intelligence which, you bet, can only lead to starvation around the New York jazz scene. Club owners hate intelligent musicians almost as much as they hate those coffee shops that are beginning to feature jazz. (For instance, I know one club owner who won't hire Cecil Taylor, but is angry that the pianist can find fitful work at the Take Three, a Village coffee house.)

But since the breakup of the first Ornette Coleman band, except for a year with Sonny Rollins, Don Cherry has had a very difficult time finding any work, even though he has been playing, and is playing now, the freshest and most powerful music to be heard on trumpet in some time. And I think it is the measure of that first Coleman band to get into

New York, that each member of it really turned out to be a major instrumentalist if not an actual innovator. Cherry, drummer Billy Higgins, bassist Charlie Haden and, of course, Ornette himself, have each helped change jazz, certainly as a group, but singly as well. And at this writing, none of them is working steadily.

When Don was with the Coleman band, he worked, as did all the other members, more or less in Ornette's shadow. Also, there was the fact that they were all playing Coleman's music, and the rest of the group's solos could only find form as statements in contrast to and extension of the dominant tone and feeling, which was Ornette's. Don's role, in this sense, was much the same as Miles Davis' on those early sides with Charlie Parker. In fact, listening to the recorded work of Coleman and Cherry immediately brings to mind the Parker-Davis collaborations, though we can only see them as collaborations now, from a distance. Bird set the initial pace and tone, and Miles responded as best he could, though that best, to my mind, seems at each rehearing even more interesting. So I think it was with Don Cherry. His responses to and interpretations of the Coleman musical genius allowed his own singular intelligence to blossom rather than wilt. It is the use the wise always make of the inspired. So that listening to Don Cherry now, the one real debt to Ornette Coleman one can hear Cherry constantly acknowledging is the intelligence of the music. Cherry is an autonomous stylist.

But being so singular a stylist, which means that a musician depends almost completely on his own personal *secret* ear as arbiter as to whether a solo is "right" or not, is the very thing that has helped estrange Don Cherry from club owners and hippies alike. Dull people are always looking for something familiar, something they've experienced before, so that they can effortlessly assimilate anything touted as "new." But the really fresh or the really singular can only baffle the listener who demands, even unconsciously, that every "new" musician sound like somebody they've already heard and digested.

People chastised Roy Eldridge because he didn't sound like Louis; then jumped on Dizzy when he showed up not sounding like Roy. Miles was spoken of rather derogatorily, I remember, because he didn't hear up in that register in which Gillespie usually does his thing. And now I've heard a man want to know why Don Cherry wasn't soft (growing softer) and given to a purple lyricism. But even so, Cherry has learned from Miles, just as Dizzy learned from Eldridge and Eldridge learned from Armstrong and Armstrong learned from Joe Oliver. But it is the use made of these learnings that is and will remain important. The things Cherry got from Miles, like the things Gillespie got from Eldridge, went to make up a different song for a very different story.

Don was born in Oklahoma in 1936, and lived in Kenner, Oklahoma, as well as Oklahoma City, before moving, at age four, to Los Angeles. His father was a bartender at the Plantation Club in L.A., which featured people like Billy Eckstine, Erskine Hawkins, etc., and he got to see the workings of a very sophisticated night life very early. "By the time I got to junior high school, my sister and I would dance at my father's parties just before we went to bed. The people would throw money, and they would give us a taste, then they'd take the rest and go out and buy a bottle.

"My grandmother married a wrestler named Tiger Nelson, who also played the piano. He used to take me with him to the various places he played. My mother had to buy me a horn. But my father didn't want me to play and get mixed up with musicians, because of the dope thing. And later on, when I started getting jobs, we'd practice for the gig and then he wouldn't let me go. Sometimes I'd have to sneak out to play."

Don learned to play almost all of the brass instruments

during his early high-school days, e.g., sousaphone and baritone. He played with a few school bands, march and dance,
as well as with several groups he organized with other young
high school jazzmen. An important catalyst to Don's musical
activities was a music teacher at Jefferson High School in
Los Angeles, Samuel Brown, who also taught Art Farmer
and young tenor man Charles Lloyd. Wardell Grey went to
Jefferson earlier. Under Mr. Brown's tutelage Jefferson High
had some of the most swinging dance bands in the area. The
band's book, while Cherry was there, included a few of
Dizzy's tunes like "Things to Come" and "Manteca," and
even some John Lewis' arrangements.

Don wasn't actually a student at Jefferson, so he had to
"ditch" the last period at his own school, in order to make
the daily practice sessions. But good jazz is irrelevant to
truant officers, and they caught the young trumpeter and
punished him. But it was at the truants' detention school
that Don met drummer Billy Higgins, who was, as Don remembers, captain of that institution's basketball team. It
was the beginning of an association that has led to some very
fine music.

About a year or so later, Don was playing diverse jobs all
over the Los Angeles area. Strangely enough, on quite a few
of the jobs he worked as a pianist. He was working on such
jobs with part of the rhythm section that helped Art Farmer
into public recognition with "Farmer's Market." Drummer
Lawrence Marable and bassist Harper Cosby also showed
Cherry how to play progressions more expertly.

Another group that Don became part of around this same
time (mid-1950's) was The Jazz Messiahs, which featured
George Newman, a young alto man whom Cherry still considers "a genius." Newman and Cherry went to grade school
together, and Newman, by the time he got into high school,
had already mastered most of the reeds and could play most
of Parker's tunes. Cherry and Newman were already going

on the road with their group when they were seventeen and eighteen and playing a good many of Newman's arrangements. When Newman left the group he was replaced by James Clay. Cherry mentions that the Jazz Messiahs were, in part, inspired because these young Negro musicians could not play in the Gompers Junior High dance band. "They were playing the 'Johnson Rag,' and wouldn't let us in . . . that's when we started playing Bird tunes."

Cherry met Ornette Coleman, as he says, "at someone's house" in Los Angeles. "Ornette's wife had all the jazz records. Hip Savoys, Dial, Prestige . . . a very good collection. And she would lend us a record, but we'd have to learn both sides of the record before we could borrow another. She played a little cello."

Coleman and Cherry played their first job together in Vancouver, Canada. "It was Ornette's first jazz gig, and he was really beautiful. I stayed up there, but Ornette went back to Los Angeles," trying to find more work and/or a way to New York. He wrote Cherry a little later on that he could get a record date ("Something Else"!!!!, Contemporary C3551), and Don came back to Los Angeles. As he puts it, "We were studying together then . . . if we weren't playing new tunes, we were playing chromatics, intervals, the elements of music."

Finally, in 1959 Cherry came to New York, and also, along with Ornette Coleman, to the School of Jazz at Lenox, Massachusetts. The music that Cherry made, as part of the Ornette Coleman quartet, on those first records, as well as during their initial appearances at the old Five Spot Cafe, already enrich the mythology of recent jazz history. And as I mentioned earlier, Cherry's work with Ornette was only the beginning, of what ought to be a fantastic career.

Recently Cherry visited me and went into some of his ideas about music, which, of course, would mean he was talking about the controlling passion of his life. A great many of the things he talked about were valuable enough to pass on. For one thing, Don is writing a book, a kind of journal of his life, in much the same way that Girolamo Cardano must have. And some of the notes I took will certainly find their way into that book.

We talked first about his recent employment with Rollins. "I heard the group (with Jim Hall, etc.) before Billy (Higgins) and I started playing with them. It was a listenable group . . . but I think the quality of the improvising got a little better after we came in. The Europe group (with Don, Billy and bassist Henry Grimes) was, I think, one of Sonny's brightest groups. Everybody was playing their horns . . . and their feelings, too.

"When everybody's got their mind and feelings in tune, it's separate from the presence of the audience. Everybody carries their brightness . . . it makes a sound.

"Separate yourself, and each time it'll be different. Be at the instant, absolute. The music will have a quality at its instant absolute. And that will be brilliant."

Don uses language the way he plays, with a preciseness based on specific insight. *Bright, brightness, brilliant, brilliance,* are words he came to again and again, hoping that his meaning was clear.

"When a group first gets together they ought to put in time learning the meaning of music. Getting control over phrases everybody's going to play together. The rhythm section has a very important thing in this . . .

"But musicians are always talking about 'my thing,' 'your thing,' when the only thing you can talk about is when everybody's in tune. All the young muscians playing now what they call freedom have to learn it, too. The group we had with Ornette was in tune. One year playing together every day did it. Playing together every day.

"It only takes two to start a group. If the two are maturely strong, and have a oneness, then the others will feel it and

touch their own sound, voice, or whatever . . . then they add
to that brightness. And the more you play together, when
the group really gets in tune, the music gets brighter, more
and more brilliant.

"Four people playing strong, really in tune with themselves. That's really something. It's counterpoint in its greatest state. One. And one covers a whole lot of space."

Cherry is presently a member of a brand new group consisting of Archie Shepp, tenor; John Tchicai, alto; Don Nelson, bass; and J. C. Moses, drums. This talk came just before
I heard the group play a concert at Harout's in the Village. I
want to say here that I think this group, if the other musicians can get drummer Moses to listen a little more, and
pretend he's Philly Joe Jones a little less, will be one of the
most exciting units anywhere. One of the tunes they played
at this initial concert was Monk's "Crepuscule with Nellie."
It was very very moving music; very powerful and very
beautiful.

This new band ought to have a pretty wild book with
Cherry, Shepp and Tchicai writing for them. Cherry and I
also talked about composing. "I don't need a piano to com-
pose. Musical composition is mathematical. You just have to be
able to hear. The sound determines where the piece will
go.

"Usually a tune will be an ear or a feeling. And the tune is
just written to get the feeling going. Or a color. Bird and
Monk sound like their kind of minds . . . and as many times
as they played a tune the actual mode is still there, but the
*reason* they play the tune might be different."

Cherry's ideas on music, or more precisely, the music he
wants to make, might seem esoteric to some, but I think it's
because Don is so determined to be a musician and an artist,
and not merely any of the more flagrantly social adaptations
of musician/hippy that seem so popular around the New
York jazz scene. Other musicians' disdain, even hostility for
what Don and some of the other young musicians are doing,

enforces a kind of dreary social ostracism, which can culmi-
nate in just such a hopeless scene as I witnessed not long ago
at the Five Spot Cafe. Cecil Taylor's drummer, Sonny Murray, asked to sit in with one of the groups that were holding
down the Monday night sessions in typically uninspired,
sloppy, but "fashionable," form. And even though it was for
the most part a "blowing session," the musicians told Murray
he couldn't make it because they had some special arrangements. It is just such arbitrary quasi-social exclusivity that
has led players like Don Cherry to find their own reasons
and techniques for making the music they feel they have to
make. Music for Cherry is not merely a way to increase his
standard of living and meet a few hungry ladies, it is the
form through which he can give us information about the
world, and his findings there.

"You really begin to get into something when you can play
what you can hum. But I never thought about playing
trumpet. I always thought about playing music. I knew my
tonsils weren't good enough. But when you get the music at
the right quality, you don't think about the instrument. I'm
not conscious of embouchure when I'm really playing. You
practice and play, strengthening your embouchure, to get
range . . . but then you have to know what to do then. A
style can be one sound. I want my playing to be musically
mature and humanly natural.

" 'Listen,' is a word I think about as much as 'music.' I'm
thankful to be a musician, but a musician ought to want to
be an artist. All an artist needs is a tool. The mistake is to use
the art itself as a tool . . . but it's not a tool, it's a being. The
musician-artist should be a master of improvising. That's the
kind of musicians I enjoy playing with. That's the kind of
musicians I've been playing with. Musicians who put a lot of
value on bringing the music alive . . . as much value as they
put on performing. There's a difference between playing and
performing. I mean playing *together*."

Even though Don has been featured on most of Ornette

Coleman's records, and is the Critics' New Star for this year, he has yet to have a record issued with himself as leader. Atlantic has one date in the can he made about two years ago with John Coltrane, Percy Heath and drummer Ed Blackwell, which they show no signs of releasing at this point, even though a lot of people are crying to hear it.* Cherry also made some tapes with a trio including Henry Grimes on bass and Blackwell, which Atlantic seems to be sitting on as well. Also, I've just heard some tapes of the new Shepp-Cherry-Tchicai group, which some record company ought to pick up on very quickly. The tapes are killers; and the date has got to be released, even if it doesn't rival the sales of "Jive Samba," etc.

Don has the humility of an artist, i.e., he knows that his goal is not some very possible "perfection" (since the completion of one statement simply reintroduces the possibility of more), but the useful expression of his human complexity in a mode that is singular and personal. Nothing is ever *finished*, except the mediocre or the pretentious. The only people who should be consistently interested in "masterpieces" are museums and other people who have no *use* for them. So that Don Cherry is constantly listening, as he said of his playing on the recent release *Ornette On Tenor*. "Blackwell sets up rhythm as a form . . . and I really couldn't play with him then . . . but now I hear just what he's doing. I used to make the sound, find out what it was, and then resolve it. But now I can feel the sound as well as hear it, and

---

* Record was finally released in 1966 called "The Avant-Garde," Atlantic, 1451, with John Coltrane, tenor and soprano saxophones; Donald Cherry, trumpet; Percy Heath, bass; Ed Blackwell, drums. And on "Cherryco" and "The Blessing," Charlie Haden plays bass.

|       (1)              |       (2)              |
| 1. "Cherryco"          | 1. "The Blessing"      |
| 2. "Focus on Sanity"   | 2. "The Invisible"     |
|                        | 3. "Bemsha Swing"      |

Recorded 1960

I am learning how to control it. When it came time for me to play, after Ornette and the others played, I used to think, Damn, what space haven't they used up? Now I'm finding out."

# 1965

## New Black Music: A Concert in Benefit of The Black Arts Repertory Theatre/School Live

*New Wave in Jazz** Impulse A-90
  (New Black Music)

> (Recorded "live" At Village Gate, New York City, March 28, 1965)

            (1)

1. "Nature Boy"
   (John Coltrane, tenor; Jimmy Garrison, bass; Elvin Jones; McCoy Tyner, piano)
2. "Holy Ghost"
   (Albert Ayler, tenor sax; Joel Freedman, cello; Lewis Worrell, bass; Donald Ayler, trumpet; Sonny Murray, drums)
3. "Blue Free"
   (Grachun Moncur, trombone; Bill Harris, drums; Cecil McBee, bass; Bobby Hutcherson, vibraphone)

            (2)

1. "Hambone"
   (Archie Shepp, tenor sax; Reggie Johnson, bass; Virgil

---

*Liner notes for *New Wave in Jazz*
  © 1965 by ABC Records, Inc.
  1330 Avenue of the Americas
  New York, New York 10019
All Rights Reserved. Used by Permission.

Jones, trombone; Marion Brown, alto sax; Roger Blank, drums; Fred Pirtle, baritone sax; Ashley Fennell, trumpet)

2. "Brilliant Corners"
(Charles Tolliver, trumpet; Cecil McBee, bass; James Spaulding, alto sax; Billy Higgins, drums; Bobby Hutcherson, vibraphone)

(Record was a concert for the benefit of The Black Arts Repertory Theater/School, and was named by me, New Black Music. A&R Director Bob Thiele saw to it, however, that NBM was a subtitle. Also, two artists that appeared at the concert were not included on the record, and this was a terrible loss, e.g., Sun-Ra and His Myth-Schience Arkestra, which included, and still includes, estimable performers like Marshall Allen, alto; John Gilmore, tenor; Pat Patrick, baritone; Ronnie Boykins, bass; and others; plus singer, Betty Carter, one of the most lyrically articulate jazz singers to show up in many moons.)

L.J.

THESE NOTES ARE made up of two parts. One part a description of what Black Art and The Black Arts are, and why the concert. The other a sequence of responses to the music itself, and what it means.

I have been writing in many places about this new black music. I have made theories, sought histories, tried to explain. But the music itself is not about any of those things. What do our words have to do with flowers? A rose is not sweet because we explain it so. We could say anything, and no rose would answer.

TRANE is now a scope of feeling. A more fixed traveler, whose wildest onslaughts are now gorgeous artifacts not even deaf people should miss.

The sway of "Nature Boy" is lyric. When Trane sounds

like what a search could sound like, we can understand that
it is now not essentially a search for what to *believe* in. *The
Peace of the Cosmos is infinite motion.*

*ALBERT AYLER* thinks that everything is everything. All
the peace. All the motion. That he is a vessel from which
energy is issued, issues. He thinks (or maybe he doesn't
think) that he is not even here. Not even here enough to be
talked about as Albert, except we *are* biological egos (we
Think). Separate. Sometimes unfeeling of each other (thing)
but Music joins us. Feeling. Art. Whatever produces a
common correspondent for existence.

Do you *understand* why this is a beautiful album?

Trane is a mature swan whose wing span was a whole new
world. But he also showed us how to murder the popular
song. To do away with weak Western forms. He is a beautiful philosopher. You would say to him, listening to his own
projection of mysticism, "That's the way it was told to me."

Albert Ayler has heard Trane, and Ornette Coleman and
has still taken the music another way. People should be re-
ferred to *Spirits, Bells, Spiritual Unity, My Name Is Albert
Ayler.*

Albert Ayler is a master of staggering dimension now, and
it disturbs me to think that it might take a long time for a lot
of people to find it out. (Except they knew it all the time,
like that other shit you can't explain.)

Trane is Oriental (Eastern) on "Nature Boy." A peace
idiom, and time, placement of himself. When he speaks of
God, you realize it is an Eastern God. Allah, perhaps.

Albert Ayler is the atomic age. Sun-Ra, who was supposed
to be heard on this album, but was not because of the mis-
sionary's vagaries, is the Space Age. These two ages are
co-existent, but all are. Trane the age of bright (mystical)
understanding. Archie Shepp, the age of cities, an urbane
traveler with good sense (heart, ear).

This album will be for many people their initial hearing of

most of these musicians. It should be, for such ears, the touchstone of the new world. There is so much here.

But the album is also heavy evidence that something is really happening. Now. Has been happening, though generally ignored and/or reviled by middle-brow critics (usually white) who have no understanding of the emotional context this music comes to life in.

This is some of the music of contemporary black culture. The people who make this music are intellectuals or mystics or both. The black rhythm energy blues feeling (sensibility) is projected into the area of reflection. Intentionally. As expression . . . where each term is equally respondent.

*Projection over sustained periods* (more time given, and time proposes a history for expression, hence it becomes reflective projection.

*Arbitrariness of form* (variety in nature).

*Intention of performance as a learning experience.*

These are categories which make reflection separate from expression; as Pure Expression/and Pure Reflection (if such categories are more than theoretically existent. Expression does not set out to instruct, but it does anyway . . . if the objects of this mind-energy are so placed that they do receive. Reflection intends to change, is a formal learning situation. But getting hit on the head with a stick can do you as much good as meditating.

In order for the non-white world to assume control, it must transcend the technology that has enslaved it. But the expression and instinctive (natural) reflection that characterize black art and culture, listen to these players, transcends any emotional state (human realization) the white man knows. I said elsewhere, "Feeling predicts intelligence."

That is, the spirit, the World Explanation, available in Black Lives, Culture, Art, speaks of a world more beautiful than the white man knows.

All that is to make clear what we are speaking of. And that

the music you hear (?) is an invention of Black Lives. (No matter the alien "harmonies" Ayler's cellist presents . . . a kind of intrepid "Classicism" that wants to represent Europe as "hip.")

Grachun Moncur represents, along with Charles Tolliver's group, the cool aspect of the new generation, the post-Milesian. The vibist, Bobby Hutcherson makes this stance thoughtful and challenging, as does, say, a drummer like Tony Williams or bassist Cecil McBee, who can stretch out even further.

These musicians change what is given and hopefully understood. What the normal feeling of adventure is. You think hard-bop to cool soft bop. But theirs is a persistent will to be original that sheds these labels effortlessly. Some of the musicians in the Tolliver/Moncur groups have played together many times on those hip Blue Note records with Jackie McLean or Andrew Hill or Wayne Shorter, etc. These are men (Jackie, the perennial strongman) who show you the music is changing before your very ears.

These, and the others I mentioned before, names names, to conjur with, no one should forget. OK, speak of them as personalities if you want to. Sonny Murray is a ghost, listen to him thrash and moan with "Holy Ghost." Listen to Louis Worrell, Charles Tyler, Don Ayler, closely because they are newer and might be telling you something you never bargained for. Listen to Trane, Ornette, Sun-Ra, Milford Graves, Tchicai, Brown. Listen to everybody beautiful. You hear on this record poets of the Black Nation.

New Black Music is this: Find the self, then kill it.

# 1967

## Sonny's Time Now

| | The Music |
|---|---|
| Sonny Murray, drums | "Virtue" |
| Albert Ayler, tenor | "Justice" |
| Don Cherry, trumpet | "Black Art" |
| Henry Grimes, bass | |
| Louis Worrell, bass | |
| LeRoi Jones reading "Black Art" | |

AT LAST Sonny Murray, the mythical red-black man from Oklahoma has an album of his own. Where he is given his long over due.

Sonny Murray, who is the innovator, the dean of new music drummers. His work with Cecil Taylor (from whom Sonny, as he willingly acknowledges, got turned on to what freedom was) first brought him awesome putdowns and worship from musicians, and the tight hard-core hippies and serious music listeners.

After leaving Cecil, Sonny stretched out in Albert Ayler's various groups. And some of Sonny's best work has been recorded with the Ayler brothers (e.g., "Bells," "Spirits Rejoice," etc.)

People have never really known what to think about Sonny. He is so purely and absolutely committed to making music, to thinking about, living within his music. "Freedom," Sonny has always said, "Free," about this music, about his playing. "I'm trying to play the music, like I feel it, Free."

Sonny makes it about *energy* and *strength*. These are keys to his method and style. Freedom, energy and strength. "To play strong, forever," is the holy man's wish. It is Sonny Murray's wish.

Watching Sonny play, as he swoops and floats, hovers, lunges, above and into the drums, it is immediate . . . his body-ness, his physicality in the music. Not just as a drum beater but as a conductor of energies, directing them this way and that way. Just scraping a cymbal this time, smashing it the next. Both feet straight out with the bass drums. His rolls and bombs the result of body-mined spirit feel. He wants "natural sounds," natural rhythms. The drum as a re-actor and manifestor of energies coursing through and pouring out of his body. Rhythm as occurrence. As natural emphasis.

You hear him moaning behind his instrument, with his other beautiful instrument. His voice. The sound of feeling. The moan, a ragged body-spasm sound, like some kind of heavy stringed instrument, lifting all the other sounds into prayers.

Playing with Sonny on this side are some of the strongest players of the new music. Albert Ayler, who is the new sound on the tenor saxophone. Indeed, Albert's weight and strength have taken the music "another way." Straight out and open, and freed and spiritual. Everybody is listening to Albert (he already has some hand-picked imitators . . . but so do all innovators, e.g., there are also a lot of Sonny Murray replicas and near replicas floating around).

Don Cherry was one of Ornette's original hatchet men. An innovator of the highest rank. (In fact the personnel of Sonny's band here is made up from side to side, not just with sidemen, but with innovators and new creators and growing

giants. Though not necessarily recognized by bagaguts
America and her freakish addiction to bullshit. But they will
be recognized by said freaks when it's time to steal from
them.)

Listen to the Cherry-Ayler duets throughout the album.
They make you slide around chortling. Don, instinctively,
placing his bullet-like metallic against wild Albert, getting
in, getting in, describing the other space. When Albert
might make you think there is no more, space. But it's freedom. You can go any where, you can.

Henry Grimes and Louis Worrell should be two of the
most famous bassists on the planet. They are among the
best. Both are startling, and in tandem, as they are on this
album, they make a droning getup sound, behind and on top
of everybody, that "collects" the music and drives it at the
same time.

This is deep music (all of these are Sonny's compositions).
It goes all through you, makes the circle of excitement and
adventure, from earth to heaven, man in between going both
ways, elliptical and perfect as anything. Get to this music,
if you can. Get to it, and it will, in turn, get to you.

# 1966

## The Changing Same (R&B
and New Black Music)

THE BLUES IMPULSE transferred . . . containing a race, and its expression. *Primal* (mixtures . . . transfers and imitations). Through its many changes, it remained the exact replication of The Black Man In The West.

An expression of the culture at its most un-self- (therefore showing the larger consciousness of a *one self*, immune to bullshit) conscious. The direct expression of a place . . . jazz seeks another place as it weakens, a middle-class place. Except the consciously separate from those aspirations. Hence the so-called avant-garde or new music, the new Black Music, is separate because it seeks to be equally separate, equally unself-conscious . . . meaning more conscious of the real weights of existence as the straightest R&B. There are simply more temptations for the middle-class Negro because he can make believe in America more, cop out easier, become whiter and slighter with less trouble, than most R&B people. Simply because he is closer to begin with.

Jazz, too often, becomes a music of special, not necessarily emotional, occasion. But R&B now, with the same help from white America in its exploitation of energy for profit, the same as if it was a gold mine, strings that music out along a similar weakening line. Beginning with their own vacuous "understanding" of what Black music is, or how it acts upon you, they believe, from the Beatles on down, that it is about white life.

*The Blues, its "kinds" and diversity, its identifying parent styles.* The phenomenon of jazz is another way of specifying cultural influences. The jazz that is most European, popular or avant, or the jazz that is Blackest, still makes reference to a central body of cultural experience. The impulse, the force that pushes you to sing . . . all up in there . . . is one thing . . . what it produces is another. It can be expressive of the entire force, or make it the occasion of some special pleading. Or it is all equal . . . we simply identify the part of the world in which we are most responsive. It is all there. We are exact (even in our lies). The elements that turn our singing into direction reflections of our selves are heavy and palpable as weather.

We are moved and directed by our total response to the possibility of all effects.

We are bodies responding differently, a (total) force, like against you. You react to push it, re-create it, resist it. It is the opposite pressure producing (in this case) the sound, the music.

The City Blues tradition is called that by me only to recognize different elements active in its creation. The slick city people we become after the exodus, the unleashing of an energy into the Northern urban situation. Wholesale.

The line we could trace, as musical "tradition," is what we as a people dig and pass on, as best we can. The call and response form of Africa (lead and chorus) has never left us, as a mode of (musical) expression. It has come down both as vocal and instrumental form.

The rhythm quartet of the last thirty years is a very obvious continuation of Black vocal tradition, and a condensation in the form from the larger tribal singing units . . . through the form of the large religious choirs (chorus) which were initially *dancers and singers,* of religious and/or ritual purpose.

Indeed, to go back in any historical (or emotional) line of ascent in Black music leads us inevitably to religion, i.e.,

spirit worship. This phenomenon is always at the root in
Black art, the worship of spirit—or at least the summoning
of or by such force. As even the music itself was that, a
reflection of, or the no thing itself.

The slave ship destroyed a great many formal art traditions of the Black man. The white man enforced such cultural rape. A "cultureless" people is a people without a
memory. No history. This is the best state for slaves; to be
objects, just like the rest of massa's possessions.

The breakdown of Black cultural tradition meant finally
the destruction of most formal art and social tradition. Including the breakdown of the Black pre-American religious
forms. Forcibly so. Christianity replaced African religions as
the outlet for spirit worship. And Christian forms were
traded, consciously and unconsciously, for their own. Christian forms were emphasized under threat of death. What
resulted were Afro-Christian forms. These are forms which
persist today.

The stripping away, gradual erosion, of the pure African
form as means of expression by Black people, and the gradual embracing of mixed Afro-Christian, Afro-American
forms is an initial reference to the cultural philosophy of
Black People, Black Art.

Another such reference, or such stripping, is an American
phenomenon, i.e., it is something that affected all of America, in fact the entire West. This, of course, is the loss of
religiosity in the West, in general.

Black Music is African in origin, African-American in its
totality, and its various forms (especially the vocal) show
just how the African impulses were redistributed in its expression, and the expression itself became Christianized and
post-Christianized.

Even today a great many of the best known R&B groups,
quartets, etc., have church backgrounds, and the music itself
is as churchified as it has ever been . . . in varying degrees of
its complete emotional identification with the Black African-

American culture (Sam and Dave, etc. at one end . . . Dionne Warwick in the middle . . . Leslie Uggams, the other end . . . and fading).

The church continues, but not the devotion (at no level of its existence is it as large, though in the poorest, most abstractly altruistic levels of churchgoing, the emotion is the devotion, and the God, the God of that feeling and movement, remains as powerful though "redistributed" somewhat).

But the kind of church Black people belonged to usually connected them with the society as a whole . . . identified them, their aspirations, their culture: because the church was one of the few places complete fullness of expression by the Black was not constantly censored by the white man. Even the asking of freedom, though in terms veiled with the biblical references of "The Jews," went down in church.

It was only those arts and cultural practices that were less obviously capable of "alien" social statement that could survive during slavery. (And even today in contemporary America, it is much the same . . . though instead of out and out murder there are hardly more merciful ways of limiting Black protest or simple statement . . . in the arts just as in any other aspect of American life.)

Blues (Lyric) its song quality is, it seems, the deepest expression of memory. Experience re/feeling. It is the racial memory. It is the "abstract" design of racial character that is evident, would be evident, in creation carrying the force of that racial memory.

Just as the God spoken about in the Black songs is not the same one in the white songs. Though the words might look the same. (They are not even pronounced alike.) But it is a different quality of energy they summon. It is the simple tone of varying evolution by which we distinguish the races. The peoples. The body is directly figured in it. "The life of the organs."

But evolution is not merely physical: yet if you can understand what the physical alludes to, is reflect of, then it will be understood that each process in "life" is duplicated at all levels.

The Blues (impulse) lyric (song) is even descriptive of a plane of evolution, a direction . . . coming and going . . . through whatever worlds. Environment, as the social workers say . . . but Total Environment (including at all levels, the spiritual).

Identification is Sound Identification is Sight Identification is Touch, Feeling, Smell, Movement. (For instance, I can tell, even in the shadows, halfway across the field, whether it is a white man or Black man running. Though Whitney Young would like to see us all run the same.)

For instance, a white man could box like Muhammad Ali, only *after* seeing Muhammad Ali box. He could not initiate that style. It is no description, it *is* the culture. (AD 1966)

*The Spirituals . . . The Camp Meeting Songs at backwoods churches . . . or Slave Songs talking about deliverance.*

The God the slaves worshipped (for the most part, except maybe the "pure white" God of the toms) had to be willing to free them, somehow, someway . . . one sweet day.

The God, the perfection of what the spiritual delivery and world are said to be, is what the worshippers sang. That perfect Black land. The land changed with the God in charge. The churches the slaves and freedmen went to identified these Gods, and their will in heaven, as well as earth.

The closer the church was to Africa, the Blacker the God. (The Blacker the spirit.) The closer to the will (and meaning) of the West, the whiter the God, the whiter the spirit worshipped. The whiter the worshippers. This is still so. And the hard Black core of America is African.

From the different churches, the different Gods, the different versions of Earth. The different weights and "classic" versions of reality. And the different singing. Different expressions (of a whole). A whole people . . . a nation, in captivity.

Rhythm and Blues is part of "the national genius," of the Black man, of the Black nation. It is the direct, no monkey business expression of urban and rural (in its various stylistic variations) Black America.

The hard, driving shouting of James Brown identifies a place and image in America. A people and an energy, harnessed and not harnessed by America. JB is straight out, open, and speaking from the most deeply religious people on this continent.

The energy is harnessed because what JB does has to go down in a system governed by "aliens," and he will probably never become, say, as wealthy, etc., that is he will never reap the *material* benefits that several bunches of white folks will, from his own efforts. But the will of the expression transcends the physical-mental "material," finally alien system-world it has to go through to allow any "benefits" in it. Because the will of the expression is spiritual, and as such it must transcend its mineral, vegetable, animal, environment.

Form and content are both mutually expressive of the whole. And they are both equally expressive . . . each have an identifying motif and function. In Black music, both identify place and direction. We want different contents and different forms because we have different feelings. We are different peoples.

James Brown's form and content identify an entire group of people in America. However these may be transmuted and reused, reappear in other areas, in other musics for different purposes in the society, the initial energy and image are about a specific grouping of people, Black People.

Music makes an image. What image? What environment

(in that word's most extended meaning, i.e., total, external and internal, environment)? I mean there is a world powered by that image. The world James Brown's images power is the lowest placement (the most alien) in the white American social order. Therefore, it is the Blackest and potentially the strongest.

It is not simply "the strongest" because of the transmutation and harnessing I spoke of earlier. This is social, but it is total. The world is a total. (And in this sense, the total function of "free music" can be understood. See, especially, H. Dumas' story in *Negro Digest* "Will the Circle Be Unbroken?" and understand the implications of music as an autonomous *judge* of civilizations, etc. Wow!)

By image, I mean that music (art for that matter . . . or any thing else if analyzed) summons and describes where its energies were gotten. The blinking lights and shiny heads, or the gray concrete and endless dreams. But the description is of a total environment. The content speaks of this environment, as does the form.

The "whitened" Negro and white man want a different content from the people James Brown "describes." They are different peoples. The softness and so-called "well being" of the white man's environment is described in his music (art) . . . in all expressions of his self. All people's are.

If you play James Brown (say, "Money Won't Change You . . . but time will take you out") in a bank, the total environment is changed. Not only the sardonic comment of the lyrics, but the total emotional placement of the rhythm, instrumentation and sound. An energy is released in the bank, a summoning of images that take the bank, and everybody in it, on a trip. That is, they visit another place. A place where Black People live.

But dig, not only is it a place where Black People live, it is a place, in the spiritual precincts of its emotional telling, where Black People move in almost absolute openness and strength. (For instance, what is a white person who walks into a James Brown or Sam and Dave song? How would he function? What would be the social metaphor for his existence in that world? What would he be doing?)

This is as true, finally, with the John Coltrane world or the Sun-Ra world. In the Albert Ayler world, or Ornette Coleman world, you would say, "well, they might just be playing away furiously at some stringed instrument." You understand?

In the Leslie Uggams world? They would be marrying a half-white singer and directing the show . . . maybe even whispering lyrics and stuff from the wings. You understand? *The song and the people is the same.*

The reaction to any expression moves the deepest part of the psyche and makes its identifications throughout. The middle-class Negro wants a different content (image) from James Brown, because he has come from a different place, and wants a different thing (he thinks). The something you want to hear is the thing you already are or move toward.

We feel, Where is the expression going? What will it lead to? What does it characterize? What does it make us feel like? What is its image? Jazz content, of course, is as pregnant.

*The implications of content.*

The form content of much of what is called New Thing or Avant-Garde or New Music differs (or seems to differ) from Rhythm and Blues, R&B oriented jazz, or what the cat on the block digs. (And here I'm talking about what is essentially *Black Music*. Although, to be sure, too often the "unswingingness" of much of the "new" is because of its association, derivation and even straight-out imitation of certain aspects of contemporary European and white Euro-American music . . . whether they are making believe they are Bach or Webern.) Avant-garde, finally, is a bad term because it also means a lot of quacks and quackers, too.

But the significant difference is, again, direction, intent, sense of identification . . . "kind" of consciousness. And that's what its about; consciousness. What are you *with* (the word Con-With/Scio-Know). The "new" musicians are self-conscious. Just as the boppers were. Extremely conscious of self. They are more conscious of a total self (or *want* to be) than the R&B people who, for the most part, are all-expression. Emotional expression. Many times self-consciousness turns out to be just what it is as a common figure of speech. It produces world-weariness, cynicism, corniness. Even in the name of Art. Or what have you . . . social uplift, "Now we can play good as white folks," or "I went to Julliard, and this piece exhibits a Bach-like contrapuntal line," and so forth right on out to lunch.

But at its best and most expressive, the New Black Music is expression, and expression of reflection as well. What is presented is a consciously proposed learning experience. (See "The New Wave.") It is no wonder that many of the new Black musicians are or say they want to be "Spiritual Men" (Some of the boppers embraced Islam), or else they are interested in the Wisdom Religion itself, i.e., the rise to spirit. It is expanding the consciousness of the given that they are interested in, not merely expressing what is already there, or alluded to. They are interested in the *unknown*. The mystical.

But it is interpretation. The Miracles are spiritual. They sing (and sing about) feeling. Their content is about feeling . . . the form is to make feeling, etc. The self-conscious (reflective, long-form, New Thing, bop, etc.) Art Musicians cultivate consciousness that wants more feeling, to rise . . . up a scale one measures with one's life. It is about thought, but thought can kill it. Life is complex in the same simplicity.

R&B is about emotion, issues purely out of emotion. New Black Music is also about emotion, but from a different place, and, finally, towards a different end. What these musicians feel is a more complete existence. That is, the digging of everything. What the wisdom religion preaches.

(But the actual New Black Music will be a larger expression. It will include the pretension of The New Music, as actuality, as summoner of Black Spirit, the evolved music of the then evolved people.)

The differences between rhythm and blues and the so-called new music or art jazz, the different places, are artificial, or they are merely indicative of the different placements of spirit. (Even "purely" social, like what the musicians want, etc.)

For instance, use of Indian music, old spirituals, even heavily rhythmic blues licks (and soon electronic devices) by new music musicians point toward the final close in the spectrum of the sound that will come. A really new, really all inclusive music. The whole people.

Any analysis of the content of R&B, the lyrics, or the total musical will and direction, will give a placement in contrast to analysis of new jazz content. (Even to the analysis of the implied vocalism of the new music: what are its intent and direction, what place it makes, etc., are concerned.) Again even the purely social, as analyzing reference, will give the sense of difference, what directions, what needs are present in the performers, and then, why the music naturally flows out of this.

The songs of R&B, for instance, what are they about? What are the people, for the most part, singing about? Their lives. That's what the New Musicians are playing about, and the projection of forms for those lives. (And I think any analysis will immediately show, as I pointed out in *Blues People*, that the songs, the music, changed, as the people did.) Mainly, I think the songs are about what is known as "love," requited and un. But the most popular songs are always a little sad, in tune with the temper of the people's lives. The extremes. Wild Joy—Deep Hurt.

The songs about unrequited, incompleted, obstructed, etc., love probably outnumber the others very easily. Thinking very quickly of just the songs that come readily to my mind, generally current, and favorites of mine (and on that other *top ten*, which is, you bet, the indication of where the minds, the people, are). "Walk On By" "Where Did Our Love Go?" "What Becomes of the Broken Hearted?" "The Tracks of My Tears," high poetry in the final character of their delivery . . . but to a very large extent, the songs are about love affairs which do not, did not, come off. For God knows how many reasons. Infidelity, not enough dough, incredibly "secret" reasons where the loved and the lover or the lovers are already separated and longing one for the other, according to who's singing, male or female. And all more precise and specific than the Moynihan Report, e.g., listen to Jr. Walker's "Road Runner." And this missed love that runs through these songs is exactly reflect of what is the term of love and loving in the Black world of America Twentieth Century.

The miss-understanding, nay, gap . . . abyss, that separates Black man and Black woman is always, over and over, again and again, told about and cried about. And it's old, in this country, to us. "Come back baby, Baby, please don't go . . . Cause the way I love you, Baby, you will never know . . . So come back, Baby, let's talk it over . . . one more time." A blues which bees older than Ray Charles or Lightnin' Hopkins, for that matter. "I got to laugh to keep from cryin," which The Miracles make, "I got to dance to keep from cryin," is not only a song but the culture itself. It is finally the same cry, the same people. You really got a hold on me. As old as our breath here.

But there are many songs about love triumphant. "I feel good . . . I got you . . . Hey!" the score, the together self, at one and in love and swinging, flying God-like. But a differently realized life-triumph than in the older more formally religious songs. The Jordans, the Promised Lands, now be cars and women-flesh, and especially dough. (Like, *power*.) There are many many songs about Money, e.g., Barrett Deems "Money," J.B.'s "I Got Money . . . now all I need is love," among so many others. But the songs are dealing with the everyday, and how to get through it and to the other side (or maybe not) which for the most part still bees that world, but on top of it, power full, and beauty full.

The older religiosity falls away from the music, but the deepest feel of spirit worship always remains, as the music's emotional patterns continue to make reference to. The new jazz people are usually much more self-consciously concerned about "God" than the R&B folks. But most of the R&B people were *really* in the church at one time, and sang there first, only to drift or rush away later.

Even the poorest, Blackest, Black people drifted away from the church. Away from a church, usually corrupted, Europeanized, or both, that could no longer provide for their complete vision of what this world ought to be, or the next. The refuge the church had provided during the early days of the Black man's captivity in America, when it was really the one place he could completely unleash his emotions and hear words of encouragement for his life here on earth. Now the world had opened up, and the church had not. But the emotionalism the church contained, and the spirit it signified, would always demand the animating life of the Black man, and as Frazier says, "The masses of Negroes may increasingly criticize their church and their ministers, but they cannot escape from their heritage. They may develop a more secular outlook on life and complain that the church and the ministers are not sufficiently concerned with the problems of the Negro race, yet they find in their religious heritage an opportunity to satisfy their deepest emotional yearnings."

(*The Negro Church in America*, E. Franklin Frazier, Shocken, 1963, p. 73.)

It was the more emotional Blacker churches that the blues people were members of, rather than the usually whiter, more middle-class churches the jazz people went to. The church, as I said, carries directly over into the secular music, which is really not secular at all. It's an old cliché that if you just change the lyrics of the spirituals they are R&B songs. That's true by and large, though there are more brazen, even whiter, strings and echo effects the blues people use that most of the spiritual and gospel people don't use. But that's changed and changing, too, and in the straight city jamup gospel, echo chambers, strings, electric guitars, all are in evidence, and Jesus is jamup contemporary, with a process and silk suit too, my man.

But the gospel singers have always had a more direct connection with the blues than the other religious singers. In fact, gospel singing is a city blues phenomenon, and Professor Thomas Dorsey, who is generally credited with popularizing the gospel form back in Chicago in the late twenties and thirties was once a blues singer-piano player named Georgia Tom, and even worked with Ma Rainey. (He was last known to be arranging for Mahalia Jackson, who with Ray Charles at another much more legitimate and powerful level, were the popularizers of Black church sound in "popular" music during the 50's.) But then so many of them, from G.T., and even before that to J.B., have all come that way.

The meeting of the practical God (i.e., of the existent American idiom) and the mystical (abstract) God is also the meeting of the tones, of the moods, of the knowledge, the different musics and the emergence of the new music, the really new music, the all-inclusive whole. The emergence also of the new people, the Black people conscious of all their strength, in a unified portrait of strength, beauty and contemplation.

The new music began by calling itself "free," and this is social and is in direct commentary on the scene it appears in. Once free, it is spiritual. But it is soulful before, after, any time, anyway. And the spiritual and free and soulful must mingle with the practical, as practical, as existent, anywhere.

The R&B people left the practical God behind to slide into the slicker scene, where the dough was, and the swift folks congregated. The new jazz people never had that practical God, as practical, and seek the mystical God both emotionally and intellectually.

John Coltrane, Albert Ayler, Sun-Ra, Pharoah Sanders, come to mind immediately as God-seekers. In the name of energy sometimes, as with Ayler and drummer Sonny Murray. Since God is, indeed, energy. To play strong forever would be the cry and the worshipful purpose of life.

The titles of Trane's tunes, "A Love Supreme," "Meditations," "Ascension," imply a strong religious will, conscious of the religious evolution the pure mind seeks. The music is a way into God. The absolute open expression of everything.

Albert Ayler uses the older practical religion as key and description of his own quest. *Spirits. Ghosts. Spiritual Unity, Angels,* etc. And his music shows a graphic connection with an older sense of the self. The music sounds like old timey religious tunes and some kind of spiritual march music, or probably the combination as a religious marching song if you can get to that. (New crusades, so to speak. A recent interview article, with Albert Ayler and his brother, trumpet player Donald Ayler, was titled "The Truth Is Marching In," and this is an excellent metaphor of where Albert and his brother Donald want to move.)

Albert's music, which he characterizes as "spiritual," has much in common with older Black-American religious forms. An openness that characterizes the "shouts" and "hollers." But having the instruments shout and holler, say a saxophone, which was made by a German, and played, as white folks call it, "legitimately" sounds like dead Lily Pons at a funeral, is changed by Ayler, or by members of any Sanctified or Holy Roller church (the blacker churches) into howling spirit summoner tied around the "mad" Black man's neck. The Daddy Grace band on 125th Street and 8th Avenue in Harlem, in the Grace Temple, is a brass band, with somewhat the same instrumentation as a European brass choir, but at the lips of Daddy's summoners, the band is "free" and makes sounds to tear down the walls of anywhere. The instruments shout and holler just like the folks. It is their lives being projected then, and they are different from the lives Telemann, or Vivaldi sought to reanimate with their music.

But James Brown still shouts, and he is as secular as the old shouters, and the new ones. With the instruments, however, many people would like them to be more securely European oriented, playing notes of the European tempered scale. While the Eastern Colored peoples' music demands, at least, that many many half, quarter, etc. tones be sounded, implied, hummed, slurred, that the whole sound of a life get in . . . no matter the "precision" the Europeans claim with their "reasonable" scale which will get only the sounds of an order and reason that patently deny most colored peoples the right to exist. To play their music is to be them and to act out their lives, as if you were them. There is then, a whole world of most intimacy and most expression, which is yours, colored man, but which you will lose playing melancholy baby in B-flat, or the *Emperor Concerto*, for that matter. Music lessons of a dying people.

Albert Ayler has talked about his music as a contemporary form of collective improvisation (Sun-Ra and John Coltrane are working in this area as well). Which is where our music was when we arrived on these shores, a collective expression. And to my mind, the *solo,* in the sense it came to be represented on these Western shores, and as first exemplified by Louis Armstrong, is very plain indication of the changed sensibility the West enforced.

The return to collective improvisations, which finally, the West-oriented, the whitened, say, is chaos, is the *all-force* put together, and is what is wanted. Rather than accompaniment and a solo voice, the miniature "thing" securing its "greatness." Which is where the West is.

The Ornette Coleman *Double Quartet* which was called *Free Jazz* was one breakthrough to open the 60's. (It seems now to me that some of bassist Charlie Mingus' earlier efforts, e.g., *Pithecanthropus Erectus*, provide a still earlier version of this kind of massive orchestral breakthrough. And called rightly, too, I think. *Pithecanthropus Erectus*, the first man to stand. As what we are, a first people, and the first people, the primitives, now evolving, to recivilize the world. And all these and Sun-Ra who seems to me to have made the most moving orchestral statements with the New Music, all seem not so curiously joined to Duke Ellington. Ellington's "KoKo" and "Diminuendo and Crescendo . . ." can provide some immediate reference to freed orchestral form.)

The secular voice seeking clarity, or seeking religion (a spirit worship) compatible with itself. They are both pushed by an emotionalism that seeks freedom. Its answering category, the definition of the freedom sought, is equally descriptive of who is playing what? If we say we want social freedom, i.e., we do not want to be exploited or have our lives obstructed, there are roots now spreading everywhere. People even carry signs, etc. There is also the "freedom" to be a white man, which, for the most part is denied the majority of people on the earth, which includes jazz players, or for that matter, blues people. The freedom to want your own particular hip self is a freedom of a somewhat different and more difficult nature.

Then, there are all kinds of freedom, and even all kinds of spirits. We can use the past as shrines of our suffering, as a poeticizing beyond what we think the present (the "actual") has to offer. But that *is* true in the sense that any clear present must include as much of the past as it needs to clearly illuminate it.

Archie Shepp is a tenor man of the new jazz, who came out (see *Archie Shepp, New Tenor*) of an American background of Black slums and white palaces. He is a Marxist playwrighting tenor-saxophone player now. His music sounds like a perculiar barrelhouse whore tip. It wavers chunks of vibrato Ben Webster Kansas City style, but turns that character actor wail into a kind of polished cry. Which, finally, if you have ever heard him speak at some public social gathering, is articulate at a very definite place in America.

Archie's is a secular music, that remains, demands secularity, as its insistence. He probably even has theories explaining why there is no God. But he makes obeisances to the spirits of ancient, "traditional," colored people ("Hambone," "The Mac Man," "The Picaninny") and what has happened to them from ancient times, traditionally, here (*Rufus, Swung, his face at last to the wind. Then his neck snapped* or *Malcolm* or *picked clean.*).

Archie is the secular demanding clarity of itself. A reordering according to the known ("The Age of Cities"). Modern in this sense. But of "modern" we must begin to ask, "What does Modern Mean?" and "What is The Future?" or "Where Does One Want To Go?" or "What Does One *Want* To Happen?" You hear in Archie's music moans that are pleas for understanding.

Cecil Taylor is also secular. He is very much an *artist*. His references determinedly Western and modern, contemporary in the most Western sense. One hears Europe and the influence of French poets on America and the world of "pure art" in Cecil's total approach to his playing. Cecil's is perhaps the most European sounding of the New Music, but his music is moving because he is still Black, still has imposed an emotional sensibility on the music that knows of actual beauty beyond "what is given."

Even though Cecil is close to what's been called Third Stream, an "integrated" Western modernism, he is always *hotter, sassier* and newer than that music. But the Black artist is most often always hip to European art, often at his jeopardy.

The most complete change must be a spiritual change. A change of Essences. The secular is not complete enough. It is not the new music, it is a breaking away from old American forms. Toward new American forms. Ornette Coleman is the elemental land change, the migratory earth man, the country blues person of old come in the city with a funkier wilder blues. Such energy forces all kinds of movement. The freshness of this Americana. A bebopier bebop, a funkier funky. But tuxedoes can be planted among such vegetation, strings and cords tied up to send the life stretched out along a very definite path. Like ivy, finally growed up fastened to an academy. No longer wild, no longer funky, but domesticated like common silence.

Ornette, Archie and Cecil. Three versions of a contemporary Black Secularism. Making it in America, from the country, the ghetto, into the gnashing maw of the Western art world. The freedom they, the music, want is *the freedom to exist in this.* (What of the New? Where?) The freedom of the given. The freedom to exist as artists. Freedom would be the change.

But the device of their asking for this freedom remains a device for asking if the actual is not achieved. Literary Negro-ness, the exotic instance of abstract cultural resource, say in one's head, is not the Black Life Force for long if we are isolated from the real force itself, and, in effect, cooled off. Cool Jazz was the abstraction of these life forces. There can be a cool avant, in fact there is, already. The isolation of the Black artist relating to, performing and accommodating his expression for aliens. Where is the returned energy the artist demands to go on? His battery (guns and engines)?

We want to please the people we see (feel with and/or for) all the time, in the respect of actual living with. Our neighbors? Our people? Who are these? Our definitions change. Our speech and projection. Is that a chick or a broad or a woman or a girl or a bird . . . or what is it? Where are you? What is this place that you describe with all your energies? Is it your own face coloring the walls, echoing in the halls, like hip talk by knowledgeable millionaires. What does a millionaire want as he passes through the eye of the needle? Can he really pass?

The New Music (any Black Music) is cooled off when it begins to reflect blank, any place "universal" humbug. It is this fag or that kook, and not the fire and promise and need for evolution into a higher species. The artist's resources must be of the strongest, purest possible caliber. They must be truest and straightest and deepest. Where is the deepest feeling in our lives? There is the deepest and most meaningful art and life. Beware "the golden touch," it will kill everything you useta (used to) love.

There are other new musicians, new music, that take freedom as already being. Ornette was a cool breath of open space. Space, to move. So freedom already exists. The change is spiritual. The total. The absolutely new. That is the absolute realization. John Coltrane, who has been an innovator of one period in jazz and a master in another period, is an example of the secular yearning for the complete change, for the religious, the spiritual.

Sun-Ra is spiritually oriented. He understands "the future" as an ever widening comprehension of what space is, even to the "physical" travel between the planets as we do anyway in the long human chain of progress. Sun-Ra's Arkestra sings in one of his songs, "We travel the spaceways, from planet to planet." It is science-fact that Sun-Ra is interested in, not science-fiction. It is evolution itself, and its fruits. God as evolution. The flow of *is*.

So the future revealed is man explained to himself. The travel through inner space as well as outer. Sun-Ra's is a new content for jazz, for Black music, but it is merely, again, the spiritual defining itself. ("Love in Outer Space," "Ankh," "Outer Nothingness," "The Heliocentric World," "When Angels Speak of Love," "Other Worlds," "The Infinity of the Universe," "Of Heavenly Things," etc., etc.) And the mortal seeking, the human knowing spiritual, and willing the evolution. Which is the Wisdom Religion.

But the content of The New Music, or The New Black Music, is toward change. It is change. It wants to change forms. From physical to physical (social to social) or from physical to mental, or from physical-mental to spiritual. Soon essences. Albert Ayler no longer wants notes. He says he wants sound. The total articulation. Ra's music changes places, like Duke's "jungle music." Duke took people to a spiritual past, Ra to a spiritual future (which also contains "Little Sally Walker . . . sitting in a saucer . . . what kind'a saucer? . . . a flying saucer").

African sounds, too; the beginnings of our sensibility. The new, the "primitive," meaning *first*, new. Just as Picasso's borrowings were Western avant-garde and "the new" from centuries ago, and Stravinsky's borrowings were new and "savage," centuries old and brand new.

The Black musicians who know about the European tempered scale (Mind) no longer want it, if only just to be contemporary. That changed. The other Black musicians never wanted it, anyway.

Change

Freedom
and finally Spirit. (But spirit makes the first two possible. A cycle, again?)

What are the qualitative meanings and implications of these words?

There is the freedom to exist (and the change to) in the existing, or to reemerge in a new thing.

Essence

How does this content differ from that of R&B.

Love, for R&B, is an absolute good. There is love but there is little of it, and it is a valuable possession. How Sweet It Is To Be Loved By You. But the practical love, like the practical church the R&B people left, a much more emotional church and spirit worship than most jazz people had, is a day-to-day physical, social, sensual love. Its presence making the other categories of human experience mesh favorably with beautiful conclusions. "Since I Lost My Baby" (or older) "When I Lost My Baby . . . I almost lost my mind." There is the object (even, the person). But what is the *object* of John Coltrane's "Love" . . . There is none. It is for the sake of Loving, Trane speaks of. As Ra's "When Angels Speak of Love."

I said before, "the cleansed purpose." The rise, the will *to be* love. The contemplative and the expressive, side by side, feeding each other. Finally, the rhythms carry to the body, the one (R&B) more "quickly," since its form definitely includes the body as a high register of the love one seeks.

The change to Love. The freedom to (of) Love. And in this constant evocation of Love, its need, its demands, its birth, its death, there is a morality that shapes such a sensibility, and a sensibility shaped by such moralizing.

Sometimes through Archie Shepp's wailing comes a dark yowl of desire in the place we are at, and for that place, to love him. And of actual flesh, that also comes through, that it is a man, perhaps crying. But he will reason it (logic as popping fingers, a hip chorus with arcane reference) down to what you hear.

Otis Redding will sing "You Don't Miss Your Water," and it is love asked for. Some warm man begging to be with a woman. Or The Temptations' "If It's Love That You're Running From" . . . there's no hiding place. . . . But the cry in Shepp's sound is not for a woman, it is a cry, a wail. But not so freed from the object, the specific, as say Trane's.

Content Analysis, total content. Musical, Poetic, Dramatic, Literary, is the analysis in total, which must come, too. But, briefly, the R&B content is usually about this world in a very practical, where we literally are, approach. Spiritual Concern, in big letters, or "Other World" would be corn or maudlin, would not serve, in most R&B, because to the performers it would mean a formal church thing. But this will change, too. Again, "I got money, now all I need is love," and that insistence will demand a clearer vision of a *new* spiritual life.

The Black Man in R&B is the Black Man you can readily see. Maybe Sadder or Happier or Swifter or Slower than the actual, as with all poetry, but that average is still where the real is to be seen. (Even the "process" on the haid is practical in a turned around way, to say, "I'monna get me some hair like that . . . blow stuff." Badge of power, etc. The more literary or bourgeois Black man would never wear his badge (of oppression) so openly. His is more hidden (he thinks). He will tell you about Mozart and Kafka, or he will tell you about Frank Sinatra and James Michener. It works out the same, to the same obstruction to self. And, finally, the conk is easier to get rid of. If you can dig that.

R&B is straight on and from straight back out of traditional Black spirit feeling. It has the feeling of an actual spontaneity and *happiness*, or at least *mastery*, at the time. Even so, as the arrangements get more complicated in a useless sense, or whitened, this spontaneity and mastery is reduced. The R&B presents expression and spontaneity, but can be taken off by the same subjection to whitening influences. A performer like Dionne Warwick (and The Supremes sometimes as well among others) with something of the light quickness of the "Detroit (Motown) Sound," treads a center line with something like grace. The strings and softness of her arrangements, and of many of her songs, are like white torch singers' delight, but her beat (she used to be a gospel singer in New Jersey) and sound take her most times into a warmth undreamed of by the whites. Though as the $$$ come in, and she leans for a "bigger audience," traveling in them circles, too, etc., then she may get even whiter perhaps. It is a social phenomenon and a spiritual-artistic phenomenon as well.

The New Black Music people, by and large, have been exposed to more white influences than the R&B people. Most of the new musicians have had to break through these whiteners to get at the sound and music they play now. That is, there is more "formal" training among the jazz people. Hence a doctrinaire whitening.

It is easier to whiten a Cecil Taylor form than a James Brown form because the Taylor form proposes to take in more influences in the first place. It sets itself up as more inclusive of what the world is. Many times it is. But this is true with any of the new forms. Finally, it depends on the activating energy and vision, where that is, how it can be got to. The new forms are many times the result of contemplation and reflection. Through these and the natural emotional outline of the performer, the new music hopes to arrive at expression and spontaneity. The R&B begins with expression and spontaneity as its ends. Which are the ends of any Black music. Though this is not to say that this is always the result. Much R&B sounds contrived and simple-minded (much of any form, for sure) because that's what is working with the sounds and forms, but what R&B proposes to be about is more readily available to us from where we are, with just what materials the world immediately has given us. The "widening" and extension, the more intellectual, new music people want many times is just funny-time shit, very very boring. That is, it may *just* be about something intellectual. The R&B might just be about something small and contrived, which is the same thing.

But the new music is consciously said to be about the mind and the spirit, as well as the heart. The beauty of an older hence "simpler" form is that it will be about the mind (and the spirit) if it is *really* about the heart. "Money won't change you . . . but time will take you out." Which can be said some other ways, but then get to them.

And Rhythm and Blues music is "new" as well. It is contemporary and has changed, as jazz has remained the changing same. Fresh Life. R&B has gone through evolution, as its singers have, gotten "modern," taken things from jazz, as jazz has taken things from R&B. New R&B takes things from old blues, gospel, white popular music, instrumentation, harmonies (just as these musics have in turn borrowed) and made these diverse elements its own.

But the Black religious roots are still held on to conspicuously in the most moving of the music. That Black emotionalism which came directly out of, and from as far back as, pre-church religious gatherings, the music of which might just be preacher to congregation, in an antiphonal rhythmic chant-poem-moan which is the form of most of the Black group vocal music that followed: Preacher-Congregation/Leader-Chorus. It is the oldest and still most common jazz form as well.

The old collective improvisation that was supposed to come out of New Orleans, with lead trumpet and clarinet weaving and trombone stunting and signifying and rhythm pounding, this form is as old as Black religious gatherings in

the forests of the West . . . and connects straight on into
Black free-Africa.

But the two Black musics—religious and secular—have
always cross-fertilized each other, because the musicians
and singers have drifted back and forth between the two
categories, with whatever music they finally came to make
being largely the result of both influences. During the De-
pression, a lot of blues people, probably most of whom had
once been in the church, "got religion" and went back (as
I've said, the church was always looked upon by Black People as a refuge, from the alien white world . . . the less it got
to be a refuge, i.e., the more it got integrated, the less hold it
had on colored people). That was a whole church era in jazz
and blues.

In the 50's during the funk-groove-soul revival, the church
music, more specifically, Gospel music, was the strongest
and healthiest influence on jazz, and R&B, too. (Grays even
opened a nightclub, The Sweet Chariot with robed hos-
tesses to make them bux off another people's ultimate concern. But nightclub, or not, they still managed to take the
music off to their own advantage.)

In fact it was the Gospel and soul-funk influence, especially as sung by Ray Charles and played by people like
Horace Silver, that "rescued" the music from the icebox of
cool jazz, which finally turned out to be a white music for
elevators, college students, and TV backgrounds. (The last
mentioned have recently got the rhythm and blues tint via
Rock'n'Roll or "Pop," i.e., the soft white "cool" forms, versions, of Gospel-derived rhythm and blues music. Which is
the way it goes.)

The cool was a whitened degenerative form of bebop. And
when mainline America was vaguely hipped, the TV people
(wizards of total communication) began to use it to make
people buy cigarettes and deodorants . . . or put life into
effeminate dicks (uhh, detectives). Then the white boys slid

into all the studio gigs, playing "their" music, for sure.

So-called "pop," which is a citified version of Rock'n'Roll (just as the Detroit-Motown Sound is a slick citified version of older R&B-Gospel influenced forms) also sees to it that those TV jobs, indeed that dollar-popularity, remains white. Not only the Beatles, but any group of Myddle-class white boys who need a haircut and male hormones can be a pop group. That's what pop means. Which is exactly what "cool" was, and even clearer, exactly what Dixieland was, complete with funny hats and funny names . . . white boys, in lieu of the initial passion, will always make it about funny hats . . . which be their constant minstrel need, the derogation of the real, come out again.

Stealing Music . . . stealing energy (lives): with their own concerns and lives finally, making it White Music (like influenzaing a shrill rites group). From anyplace, anytime to "We all live in a yellow submarine," with all their fiends, etc., the exclusive white . . . *exclusive* meaning *isolated* from the rest of humanity . . . in the yellow submarine, which shoots nuclear weapons. (Content analysis . . . lyrics of white music show equally their concerns, lives, places, ways, to death.) In the yellow submarine. Chances are it will never come up.

They steals, minstrelizes (but here a minstrelsy that "hippens" with cats like Stones and Beatles saying, "Yeh, I got everything I know from Chuck Berry," is a scream dropping the final . . . "But I got all the dough . . .") named Animals, Zombies, in imitation (minstrel-hip) of a life style as names which go to show just what they think we are . . . Animals, Zombies, or where they finally be, trying to be that, i.e., Animals, Zombies, Beatles or Stones or Sam the Sham for that matter, and not ever Ravens, Orioles, Swallows, Spaniels or the contemporary desired excellence of Supremes, Miracles, Imperials, Impressions, Temptations, etc., . . . get to them names.

Actually, the more intelligent the white, the more the

realization he has to steal from niggers. They take from us all the way up the line. Finally, what is the difference between Beatles, Stones, etc., and Minstrelsey. Minstrels never convinced anybody they were Black either.

The more adventurous bohemian white groups sing songs with lyric content into where white bohemian poets moved long ago, as say the so-called psychedelic tunes, which may talk about drugs (LSD, Psylocibin, etc.) experience, and may be also shaped by so-called RagaRock (Indian-influenced) or Folk-Rock (i.e., Rock songs with more socially conscious content). Bob Dylan, Fugs, Blues Project, Mothers, etc. But in awe of the poetic-psychedelic and LSD, the chemical saviour of grays. They hope to evolve (as the rest of us) "thru chemistry," which sounds like Dupont. The "widening of the consciousness" type action into a higher sense of existent life, and thereafter, maybe stop stealing and killing, etc., etc., etc.

The Black tip for them is a super-live life thing as well. To "Get more than we got" kind of thing. The music . . . lyrics, with instructions to "tune in, turn on, drop out" and sound an Electronic Indian Raga . . . as a meditative eclipse of present reality, a yoga saddhu pop. But in play will still drop out of their society like new Beat thing. Out of it! Yeh. But what to do about what ain't out of it. Like there are people dying, etc. Bullshit.

But the content of some anti-Viet anti-Bad stuff is a generalizing in passionate luxurious ego demonstration to be good anyway though they exists as super-feelers of their evil cement head brothers, and as flexible copout, to be anything, finally, anything but what they patently are. That is, Fugs, Freaks, Mothers, Dylan, etc. Yet it still bees white kids playing around. Dylan's "Blowin in the Wind," which is abstract and luxury playing around stuff with him, is immediately transformed when Stevie Wonder sings it because it becomes about something that is actual in the world and is substantiated by the life of the man singing it. That is, with Dylan it seems just an idea. A sentiment. But with Wonder (dig the name! and his life-style and singing is, of course, more emotional, too) you dig that it is life meant. In life.

The "new content" of white pop was protest, and with that "widening consciousness" as opposed to jes' love. But it is just this love that the white pop cannot sing about because it is not only sweet, stupid, maudlin, but now, frankly cannot be believed. Nobody can be made to believe they could love anybody. So the move.

The superficial advance. The liberal cool protest. Viet. Oh. Viet-Rock. Yeh. LBJ ain't no good. Yeh. But what, what? will happen $$$$$$ . . . stealin' all from the niggers and they bees starvin' all the time. While crooks is good and hates war, for dough. (Wins either way!)

But the "protest" is not new. Black people's songs have carried the fire and struggle of their lives since they first opened their mouths in this part of the world. They have always wanted a better day. During the socially-conscious thirties, after the city and the social sophistication of white protest movements was acquired, so-called Folk Music was the most ubiquitous Black or near-Black music in the American mainstream. This is the reason "Folk" has been associated with protest. White people saddled that horse with trade unionism, IWW, Spanish Civil War, in the same way the folk-rockers, etc. do today.

Black religious music has always had an element of protest in it. In the so-called "invisible institution," or pre-church worship of the Black slaves, the songs were about freedom, though most times couched in the metaphorical language of the Bible, substituting Jews, etc. for themselves, to escape massa's understanding.

But with secular music, integration (meaning the harnessing of Black energy for dollars by white folks, in this case in the music bizness) spilled the content open to a generalizing that took the bite of specific protest out. ("You know you cain't sell that to white folks.")

Early blues is full of talk about Black people and their exact up-hill lives. In fact you can tell an early blues tune if the word "Black" is even mentioned. Or "white" for that matter. The slickening money process shaved a lot of exactness in one area. They talk of love, and that is exact, but as a preacher said, "Today we're gonna talk about Love. I was gonna talk about Truth, but I figured I might offend somebody. So today we're gonna talk about Love." If you can dig that.

But the cycle will turn round. The more bohemian white people's desire to be at least in a recognizable world of war and stuff will be passed around to Black people, as legitimate part of the music bizness. (Just as the quickest way to get Black people to dig Africa, wear African clothes etc., is to let B. Altman's sell it, it would seem to white people, then watch all the hippies show up like they are worshipping some Orisha.)

Stevie Wonder with Dylan's "Blowin in the Wind" is a case in point. Now James Brown with his social consciousness of "Don't Be a Dropout." Specific, but civil-servant stuff, nevertheless. The Impressions' "Keep On Pushin" or Martha and The Vandellas' "Dancing in the Street" (expecially re: summer riots, i.e., "Summer's here . . .") provided a core of legitimate social feeling, though mainly metaphorical and allegorical for Black people. But it is my thought that soon, with the same cycle of the general "integrated" music bizness, the R&B songs will be more socially oriented. (*Black and Beautiful*, Jihad Singers. I'm reminded that a few years ago, Ben E. King and a few others . . . *Spanish Harlem*, etc. . . . had made a special placement of social music, but that was largely picked up by grays.)

Note: *Let the new people take care of some practical bi-ness and the R&B take care of some new bi-ness and*

*the unity musick, the people-leap, can begin in*
*earnest.*

Social consciousness in jazz is something again because it
is largely a purely instrumental music . . . though there have
always been musicians who have been deeply conscious of
their exact placement in the social world, or at least there
was a kind of race pride or consciousness that animated the
musicians and their music (again, here, Ellington is a giant.
"Black Beauty," "Black, Brown and Beige," "For My People"
and so many many others).

In recent times musicians like Charles Mingus (dig "Fable
of Faubus," etc.), Max Roach and some others have been
outspoken artists on and off the stage, using their music as
eloquent vehicles for a consciousness of self in America. The
new musicians have been outspoken about the world
through their music and off the stage as well. Archie Shepp
has perhaps been the most publicized of the new socially
conscious musicians. And some of his music is self-consciously socially responsive, e.g., "Malcolm," but this so-
called consciousness is actually just a reflection of what a
particular generation is heir to, and their various responses
from wherever they (are) find themselves.

Also, of course, the music is finally most musicians'
strongest statement re: any placement of themselves socially. And the new music, as I have stated before about
Black music, is "radical" within the context of mainstream
America. Just as the new music begins by being free. That is,
freed of the popular song. Freed of American white cocktail
droop, tinkle, etc. The strait jacket of American expression
*sans* blackness . . . it wants to be freed of that temper, that
scale. That life. It screams. It yearns. It pleads. It breaks out
(the best of it). But its practitioners sometimes do not. But
then the vibrations of a feeling, of a particular place, a
conjunction of world spirit, some of everybody can pick up

on. (Even imitate, which is Charlie McCarthy shouting freedom! or white snick workers going back to Jumpoff Manor after giving a few months to "The Problem.") It is an ominous world all right. You can say *spiritual*. You can say *Freedom*. But you do not necessarily have to be either one. If you can dig it. White, is abstract. A theory. A saying. A being . . the verb . . . the energy itself, is what is beautiful, is what we want, sometimes, are.

Music as the consciousness, the expression of where we are. But then Otis Redding in interviews in *Muhammad Speaks* has said things (or Shakey Jake, for that matter) more "radical," Blacker, than many of the new musicians. James Brown's screams, etc., are more "radical" than most jazz musicians sound, etc. Certainly his sound is "further out" than Ornette's. And that sound has been a part of Black music, even out in them backwoods churches since the year one. It is just that on the white man's instrument it is "new." So, again, it is just life need and interpretation.

Sun-Ra speaks of evolution of the cosmic consciousness; that is future, or as old as *purusa*. Where man will go. "Oh you mean space ships?" Which is like the Zen monk answering the student's question about whether or not dogs have souls . . . i.e., "Well, yes . . . and no."

And the social consciousness displayed in that music. Pharoah Sanders will say OMMMMMMMMMMMMMMMM MMMMMMMMMMMMMMMMMMMMMMMMMMMMMMMMM MMMMMMMMMMMMMMMMMMMMMMMMMM. Which is more radical than sit-ins. We get to Feel-Ins, Know-Ins, Be-Ins.

But here is a theory stated just before. That what will come will be a *Unity Music*. The Black Music which is jazz and blues, religious and secular. Which is New Thing and Rhythm and Blues. The consciousness of social reevaluation and rise, a social spiritualism. A mystical walk up the street to a new neighborhood where all the risen live. Indian-African anti-Western-Western (as geography) Nigger-sharp Black and strong.

The separations, artificial oppositions in Black Music resolved, are the ditty strong classic. (Ditty bop.) That is, the New Black Music and R&B are the same family looking at different things. Or looking at things differently. The collection of wills is a simple unity like on the street. A bigger music, and muscle, for the move necessary. The swell of a music, of action and reaction, a seeing, thrown in swift slick tone along the entire muscle of a people. The Rhythm and Blues mind blowing evolution of James-Ra and Sun-Brown. That growth to include all the resources, all the rhythms, all the yells and cries, all that information about the world, the Black ommmmmmmmmmmmmmmmm, opening and entering.

# A Brief Discography of New Music

**ORNETTE COLEMAN**
*Something Else!* (Contemporary M 3551)
*This Is Our Music* (Atlantic 1353)
*Change of the Century* (Atlantic 1327)
*The Shape of Jazz to Come* (Atlantic 1317)
*Free Jazz* (Atlantic 1364)

**JOHN COLTRANE**
*My Favorite Things* (Atlantic 1361)
*Giant Steps* (Atlantic 1311)
*Ascension* (Second Version) (Impulse A-95)
*Meditations* (Impulse A-9110)

**SONNY ROLLINS**
*What's New* (Victor LSP-2572)
*Our Man In Jazz* (Victor LSP-2612)

**CECIL TAYLOR**
*Looking Ahead!* (Contemporary M3562)
*The World of Cecil Taylor* (Candid 8006)
*Unit Structures* (Blue Note 4237)
*Into the Hot* (Impluse A-9)

**ERIC DOLPHY**
*Out There* (Prestige/New Jazz 8252)
*Eric Dolphy at the Five Spot* (Prestige/New Jazz 8260)
*(Free Jazz)* (See Coleman)

ALBERT AYLER
  *Bells* (ESP 1010)
  *Spirits Rejoice* (ESP 1020)
  *Spiritual Unity* (ESP 1002)
  *Ghosts* (Fontana 688)
  *Spirits* (Debut 146)

ARCHIE SHEPP
  *Four for Trane* (Impluse A-71)
  *Fire Music* (Impluse A-86)
  *On This Night* (Impulse A-97)

SUN-RA
  *Art Forms of Dimensions Tomorrow* (Saturn 9956)
  *The Magic City* (Saturn LP B-711)
  *The Heliocentric Worlds of Sun-Ra* (ESP-1014) Vol 1
  *The Heliocentric Worlds of Sun-Ra* (ESP-1017) Vol 2
  *Secrets of the Sun* (Saturn 5786)

SONNY MURRAY
  *Sonny's Time Now* (Jihad 663)

MILFORD GRAVES-DON PULLEN
  *At Yale University* (PG286)

VARIOUS ARTISTS (Coltrane, Shepp, Ayler, Tolliver, Moncur, Hutcherson, Murray, Brown, Jones, Higgins, Spaulding,
etc., etc.)
  *The New Wave in Jazz* (Impulse A-90)

GRACHAN MONCUR
  *Evolution* (Blue Note 4153)

NEW YORK CONTEMPORARY FIVE
  *Recorded Live at Jazzhus Montmarte* (Sonet SLP 36) Vol 1

NEW YORK ART QUARTET
  *New York Art Quartet* (ESP 1004)

# INDEX

# A Note About the Author

LeRoi Jones was born in Newark, New Jersey in 1934. A member of a lower middle-class Negro family, Mr. Jones went to "integrated" (mostly white) schools until his transfer from Rutgers to Howard University. After service in the Air Force, Mr. Jones received his M.A. in comparative literature from Columbia University. He began the poetry magazine *Yugen* and became poetry editor of Corinth Books. He has taught creative writing at the New School and at Columbia University. He is the author of: *Home: Social Essays; The System of Dante's Hell; Dutchman and The Slave; Dead Lecturer; Blues People; Moderns: New Fiction in America;* and *Preface to a Twenty Volume Suicide Note.*